Israel's Love Affair
with God

First Edition 1993

Trinity Press International
P.O. Box 851
Valley Forge, PA 19482-0851

Cover design by Brian Preuss
Cover art: *Purple Current* by Suzanne R. Neusner

Library of Congress Cataloging-in-Publication Data

Neusner, Jacob, 1932–
    Israel's love affair with God : Song of songs / Jacob Neusner.
      p.   cm. — (The Bible of Judaism library)
    Contains an "analytical translation" of Song of Songs Rabbah.
    Includes bibliographical references and index.
    ISBN 1-56338-052-8
    1. Midrash rabbah. Song of Solomon—Criticism, interpretation, etc. 2. Bible. O.T. Song of Solomon— Commentaries. I. Midrash rabbah. Song of Solomon. English. 1993. II. Title. III. Series.
BM517.M72N48   1993
296.1'4—dc20   93-18503
                                      CIP

Printed in the United States of America

93 94 95 96 97   6 5 4 3 2 1

Israel's Love Affair with God

Song of Songs

Jacob Neusner

The Bible of Judaism Library

Trinity Press International
Valley Forge

Table of Contents

If she is a wall, we will build upon her a battlement of silver;
but if she is a door, we will enclose her
with boards of cedar. (8:9)
I was a wall, and my breasts were like towers;
then I was in his eyes as one who brings peace. (8:10)
page 99

10
Symbol and Theology in Judaism

The Bible of Judaism Library Series Foreword

All three heirs to ancient Israel's holy writings—Islam, Christianity, and Judaism—revere, in addition to scripture, other scriptures or traditions: the Quran, the New Testament, and the corpus of the oral Torah, respectively. All three also maintain that the sense of these subsequent messages from God infuses the original writings. So the scriptures held in common form a principal arena of confrontation; they can, however, also provide the occasion for dialogue with each biblical religion contributing a sense unique to itself for the illumination of the others' readings of the same writings. While "Judaism," "Christianity," and "Islam" encompass religious systems of considerable diversity, all Judaisms differ from all Christianities and Islams in their reading of those scriptures. If we want to understand the religions of monotheism, therefore, we have to grasp how each has received and read ancient Israel's scriptures. Comparison begins on the foundations of what is shared, which for Judaism and Christianity is the written Torah or Old Testament. The task of comparison defines the first step toward mutual understanding and respect within a single agendum: here we differ, there we concur.

Traditions that cannot even agree on the enumeration of the years—whether from the creation of the world (as in Judaism) or from the advent of Christ (as in Christianity) or from the Hegira (as in Islam)—can hardly be expected to agree on much else. Because these traditions do agree on the sacred standing of ancient Israel's scriptures, this represents a starting point for conversation in a rational and orderly spirit. After all, Judaism, Christianity, and Islam agree on what is most important of all: that there is one God, creator of heaven and earth, whom alone we worship, by whom alone we are judged, and who has spoken to us uniquely in the scriptures of ancient Israel. We do well to read one another's reading of that common scripture. To the task of forming a spirit of cooperation among the monotheist religions, then, I dedicate this library of how Judaism reads the ancient Israelite scriptures.

By "Judaism," I mean the Judaism of the dual Torah which conceives that at Mount Sinai God gave to Moses, our rabbi, the Torah—God's will for humanity, exhaustive and whole—in two media, written and oral. The written Torah is in the Hebrew scriptures that Christianity knows as the Old Testament. The oral Torah was handed on from Moses to Joshua, the prophets, and finally to the sages at the end of a long chain of tradition. The latter produced the writings we now possess under the name of the Mishnah (ca. 200 C.E.), which is amplified in three further writings: the Tosefta (ca. 300 C.E.) and the two Talmuds—the Talmud of the land of Israel (ca. 400 C.E., "the Jerusalem Talmud" or "the Yerushalmi") and the Talmud of Babylonia (ca. 600 C.E., "the Bavli"). Along with the Mishnah and its expansions in the commentaries of the Tosefta and the two Talmuds, these same sages produced expansions and commentaries on the written Torah. These are Midrash-compilations, that is, compilations of exegeses of scripture.

The books of the Hebrew scriptures that received such amplifications were those that figured prominently in synagogue liturgy, being read either from week to week, as in the case of the Pentateuch or Five Books of Moses (Genesis, Exodus, Leviticus, Numbers, Deuteronomy), or on festival occasions in that same liturgical year. Chief among the former are Genesis Rabbah to Genesis (ca. 450 C.E.); Sifra to Leviticus (ca. 300 C.E.); Leviticus

Rabbah, also to Leviticus (ca. 450 C.E.); Sifré to Numbers (ca. 300 C.E.); and Sifré to Deuteronomy (ca. 300 C.E.). Addressed to liturgical high points in the year are Pesiqta deRab Kahana (ca. 500 C.E.), which is organized around sabbaths bearing a particular distinction and Song of Songs Rabbah, Lamentations Rabbati, Esther Rabbah, and Ruth Rabbah—all of them reaching closure at about the same time as the Talmud of Babylonia, ca. 600 C.E. These are read on the occasions of Passover, the ninth of Ab (commemorating the destruction of the Temple in 586 B.C.E. and 70 C.E., the expulsion of the Jews from Spain in 1492, and other mournful days), Purim, and Pentecost, respectively.

In the first six titles of this library, I set forth a representative sample of the way in which, in its definitive writings, the Judaism of the dual Torah received the Hebrew scriptures and turned all of them into components of its Torah. My goal is to help readers open the Midrash-compilations on their own, guided by the rules of reading set forth here, and find the modes of reading and writing intelligible with scripture in other parts of the compilations I present.

Specifically, then, we address exemplary passages of six of the great liturgical responses to scripture: two of the Pentateuchal books, Genesis and Leviticus, and four of the scrolls read on special occasions in the synagogue, Esther, Lamentations, Ruth, and the Song of Songs. It is upon the classical writings of that Judaism, which took shape in the first seven centuries of the common era (C.E. = A.D.), that every Judaic system today draws in abundance. Consequently, when we know how, in its formative age, the Judaism of the dual Torah read scripture, we gain access to the way in which, through the centuries since that time, the Hebrew scriptures entered the dual Torah that formed the theology and law of Judaism. Within Judaism, the name of that Judaism is simply "the Torah," as in "the Torah teaches" or "the Torah commands."

What we want to know in these Midrash-compilations concerns the way in which scripture makes its entry into the Torah. That formulation will strike readers as curious since, after all, everyone knows scripture (once more, "the Old Testament" or "the written Torah") is the Torah. But that formulation of matters—how scripture enters the Torah—is native to Judaism since, as we realize, Judaism conceives "the Torah" to encompass tradition in addition to scripture—Torah in an oral as well as in a written medium of formulation and transmission. While the written Torah enjoys a privileged position within the Torah, it forms only part of the Torah and not the whole of it. Hence it is quite correct to ask how scripture is received within the Torah.

Each of the scriptural books that undergoes the reading of a Midrash-compilation yields its own message; none of the Midrash-compilations emerges as a mere paraphrase of the plain sense of scripture itself. There was no conception of a historical, limited, particular plain sense that stood in judgment on fanciful and figurative senses of an other-than-historical, one-time meaning. Hence, when our sages read the story of Jacob and Esau as the tale of Israel and Rome in the time of the Christian emperors, they did not conceive that theirs was a reading distinct from the author's original intention. And how could such a conception have taken root when, after all, they knew that the oral and written Torah came from God to Moses or was the work of the Holy Spirit or otherwise transcended the particularities of time, space, and circumstance? What people today mean by "plain" or "original" meaning of scripture, for our sages corresponded to God's intent. No one, then or now, can imagine that God spoke only to one time or place or circumstance or person. God spoke everywhere and all the time, eternally, to Israel. Our sages mediated that statement to the Israel of their time and place. The framers of the Midrash-compilations wrote through scripture, with scripture, about scripture—that is how they made their statement of the Torah, oral and written, in a cogent way. That dual mode of discourse—about and through scripture, on the one side, with their own words and through available compositions, on the other—accounts for the way in which they expressed themselves.

Scripture provided language not only in the concrete sense of verses but also in the figurative sense. Regarding the latter, scripture made available stories, heroes, events, attitudes—the entire repertoire of convention in thought and conviction. Writing with scripture meant appealing to the facts that scripture provided to prove propositions that the authorships at hand wished to prove. As a mode of discourse, it required forming out of scripture the systems these writers proposed to construct. In dialogue with scripture, these writers made important statements, some of them paraphrases of scriptural lessons, others entirely their own. In the aggregate, our authorship turned to scripture not principally for prooftexts, let alone for pretexts, to say whatever they wanted. They read scripture because they wanted to know what it said, but they took for granted that it spoke to them in particular. No other premise of the focus of scriptural discourse was possible or ever entertained.

But scripture always remained separate, always marked off. The language of the Hebrew scriptures differed from the language of the Mishnah and Midrash-compilations, thus presenting us with two varieties of Hebrew. Moreover, the citation of a verse of scripture is commonly introduced by "as it is said" or "as it is written," or is otherwise distinguished by its position in a larger composition so that a clear frontier delineates scripture from Midrash. In the language of contemporary literary criticism, the Midrash-writings were in no way "intertextual," but all of the writings of the Judaism of the dual Torah other than scripture stood in an intratextual relationship to scripture. So we may say that the founders of Judaism engaged in dialogue with the scriptures of ancient Israel. This was a dialogue of their own design on a program of topics of their own concern for a purpose of their own choosing. Whether their statement accorded with the position of scripture on a given point or merely provided the simple and obvious sense of scripture or found ample support in prooftexts—none of these considerations bears material consequence.[1] What matters in the interpretation of the document is the document's own problem: how and why did those who compiled these materials consider that they made a statement not of their own but of truth? The answer, as we shall see, is that they selected and arranged what they inherited, and they framed and shaped what they themselves made up for their document so as to make in their own words and in scripture's words a single proposition that they—with complete justification—identified with both themselves and with scripture.

The ancient rabbis read scripture as God's personal letter to them. In the Midrash-compilations laid out in these pages, we find an example of how, when faced with challenge from without and crisis from within, the sages found in scripture the wisdom and the truth that guided them. No wonder, then, that these same figures undertook to answer the letter with a letter of their own. In these books we peer over their shoulders to read the letter they wrote back: their response to God's message to them, this morning, here and now. Here is no work of mere historical interest but a heritage of vital religious faith. When we encounter how our sages read and answered God's letter to them, those of us who revere scripture as God's word and who open scripture in our quest for God (in the language of Judaism, who come to the Torah to learn God's will) find a model for ourselves.

My goal is to open up for contemporary faith yet another route to Sinai: the one explored by the sages of Judaism who received the Torah as God's letter to each of them, personally, this morning. We share that response to scripture—God's personal message for today—we who open scripture today as in ages past and all time to come, because it is how and where we find God. If this library succeeds in its mission, faithful Jews and Christian will renew for themselves a program of Bible study that brings to scripture profoundly religious concerns in place of the presently prevailing program of historical and philological research. No one dismisses as inconsequential the results of scholarship, for the informed exegesis of words and phrases and sentences of scripture, not to mention the contexts to which those sentences made their statement, draws upon those results. But scholarship does not deliver scripture into our hands, and scholarship does not teach lessons of transcendence such as the Torah teaches. Scholarship in biblical studies provides inert information; faith makes Scripture live and, with it, the results of scholarship too. So let us get our perspective in line with the facts of faith. In this library we see how faithful Judaic sages accomplished that reading, and it was their reading of scripture, not a this-worldly historical or philological reading, that endowed scripture with sanctity and authority through the ages to our own day.

Notes

1. To be sure, these considerations form part of the massive system of theological apologetics created for Judaism in modern times: e.g., Judaism, not Christianity, states "the plain meaning of scripture" so that Isaiah could not possibly have been referring to Jesus Christ. But the history of modern and contemporary thought of Judaism is not at issue in this library of Judaism's reading of scripture, nor is the question of whether the sages set forth the plain meaning of scripture relevant

at all. The concept of a plain, historical, and inherent meaning, distinct from the fanciful ones invented by the Midrash-exegetes, is purely anachronistic. See Raphael Loewe, "The 'Plain' Meaning of Scripture in Early Jewish Exegesis," in *Papers of the Institute of Jewish Studies, London,* vol. 1 (1989; reprint, Lanham, Md.: University Press of America/Brown Classics in Judaica Series), 140–85. The concept of a " 'plain' meaning" demonstrates a profound misunderstanding of rabbinic literature.

Preface

The sages made use of scripture by making it their own and making themselves into the possession of scripture—a reciprocal process in which both were changed, each into the likeness and image of the other. They did this by effecting their own selections and shaping a distinctive idiom of discourse, all the while citing, responding to, and reflecting upon scripture's own words in its own context and for its own purpose—the here and now of eternal truth. Through Song of Songs, our authorship not only wrote with scripture but set forth a statement that was meant to be coherent and proportioned, well crafted and well composed. Since that statement concerned the distinctively theological question of God's and Israel's relationship, we must classify the writing as theological and find out how, in the compilation before us, the structure accomplished the authorship's goals. This volume of the Bible of Judaism Library aims at doing just that.

My translation of Song of Songs Rabbah is the second translation, closely following the first and excellent translation by

Maurice Simon, "Song of Songs," in *Midrash Rabbah*, vol. 9, ed. H. Freedman and Maurice Simon (London: Soncino Press, 1939).[1] In the body of my translation, when I use Simon's translation verbatim, I signify it this way: [Simon, p. 00]. What follows is his translation, word for word or nearly so, until the opening of a new unit of thought. Even when I do not follow Simon verbatim, I try to give credit for what I have learned from him. Where I translate in my own words but follow the sense given by Simon, I signify that as well, e.g., by inserting the words: [following Simon, p. 00]. Finally, I often absorb his versions of scriptural verses with ad hoc revisions or copy his translation of verses verbatim. Why, then, have I retranslated the document as I have?

As I explain in more general terms in *Translating the Classics of Judaism: In Theory and in Practice,* Brown Judaic Studies (Atlanta: Scholars Press, 1989), his translation—in common with all other classics of Judaism that reached closure in late antiquity—is primarily useful as a reference regarding the contents of the document. Simon tells us what is in Song of Songs Rabbah, but he does not help us study the document in any important way. His descriptive translation, lacking analytical indicators, does not make possible study of the indicative traits of the document, definition of the compilation, or analysis of the patterns of rhetoric and logic that characterize this particular piece of writing. My translation, however, makes possible these analytical studies. By isolating the smallest whole units of thought, then showing how they comprise propositional discourse, by highlighting the formal traits of the original through fixed formulas in English, my translation allows for critical inquiry that a translation lacking a reference system does not.

An analytical translation is one in which I make immediately visible to the naked eye the principal and indicative literary traits of the Hebrew, highlighting the distinctive character of rhetoric and logic of the original. I paragraph whole units of thought, from the smallest building blocks of discourse upward, and indicate the larger compositions, their beginnings and endings. On the basis of that presentation, readers may perform their own form-analyses, inquiries into modes of logical discourse, and other studies that tell us, in aesthetics as much as in theology, the authorship's message and meaning. For any distinction between method and message or form and meaning obliterates the power of discourse attained in this compilation, as in any other component of the canon of Judaism. The foundation of my analytical translation is its reference system. My reference system allows identification of each complete unit of thought or other irreducible minimum of discourse, for example, a verse of scripture. On that basis we may clearly see the formal traits of each composite or composition. Once I have the Roman numeral for a given complete unit of material, I divide it as follows: I signify the principal components of a given chapter, of which there may be only one of two. *This is indicated by an Arabic numeral, thus XIII:i.1 alludes to the first major division of the thirteenth chapter of the book. The Arabic numeral then identifies what I conceive to be a complete argument, proposition, syllogism, or fully worked out exegetical exercise (a whole thought). Finally, with a letter, A, B, C, I point to what I maintain is the smallest whole unit of thought—for example, a sentence or a major component of a sentence, a verse of scripture, a constituent clause of a complex thought, and the like.* This is indicated by a letter. Hence *I:i.1.A* alludes to the opening whole unit of thought, in the case at hand, the citation of the base verse.

As to the sources of biblical verses, I reproduce the complete translation of the Song of Songs = Song of Solomon in *The Oxford Annotated Bible with the Apocrypha: Revised Standard Version*, ed. Herbert G. May and Bruce M. Metzger (New York: Oxford University Press, 1965). I also consulted *Tanakh: A New Translation of The Holy Scriptures according to the Traditional Hebrew Text* (Philadelphia: Jewish Publication Society, 1985). Many of the translations of verses of scripture are Simon's, where he has rendered a verse in a way that immediately makes clear the intent of the exegete.

The idea for this library came to me in my teaching at the University of South Florida. In a course, "The Classics of Judaism," I found that my available textbooks on Midrash, along with all others, failed to walk the students through a passage line by line. I referred to the passage whole and complete, as though its workings were self-evident and readily accessible. The students came to class prepared, having done their reading, yet puzzled by what

they had read. When we worked our way through a passage together, however, the power and glory of the Midrash-writing
dawned. I realized that to afford students immediate access to
Midrash-writings (as far as that is possible in a language other
than the original Hebrew), a different approach from the one I
had taken in my prior textbooks and anthologies had to be explored. Specifically, I would have to explain how the literature is
put together, line by line; it does not suffice merely to translate
it into reasonably accessible American English. I would have to
concentrate on the reader rather than on the problem of the document and the genre of writing in it, such as occupied my prior
presentations of these writings. That approach governs here. If it
succeeds, readers should find the Midrash-passage clear and elo-
qent on their own. That is why nothing in these pages goes over
the problems that I address in my earlier works.[2]

My debt to my dear friend and co-worker, Dr. Harold Rast,
publisher and editor of Trinity Press International, has accumulated now for decades. It suffices to state very simply that he gives
academic religious publishing the good name that is deserves.
He and his colleagues at the other principal academic religious
presses in this country have contributed to the shaping of religious dialogue among informed and literate believers to a degree
that, to my knowledge, has no counterpart in any other country
in the world.

I express thanks also to my friends and colleagues at the University of South Florida. The Department of Religious Studies
has provided ideal circumstances in which to teach and study, and
I have found life here more productive than I had imagined possible. In times of exceptional financial rigor, the administration of
the University of South Florida has found it possible to support
my research through provision of special funds and also through
the remarkably generous terms of my appointment as Distinguished Research Professor of Religious Studies. It remains my
task to be worthy of such opportunities. In times past or even today, I do not think that many scholars have enjoyed as favorable
a situation as USF has made for me.

Since I discuss my work from day to day with Professor William Scott Green of the University of Rochester, since the idea of
"writing with scripture" was born in conversations with him, and

since the phrase itself is his, I am happy to point also to his fundamental contributions to this work and to the library of which it
forms the first volume.

Jacob Neusner
July 28, 1992
My sixtieth birthday

Notes

1. Like Simon, I translate the standard printed text. There is no other at
this time. I have never conceived that the task of a translator begins with
the establishment of "the critical text." Let the text scholars give us their
superior versions with adequate commentaries as to variants, meanings
of words, and parallel versions, and we shall happily (re)translate the
documents quite faithfully.

2. *Invitation to Midrash: The Working of Rabbinic Bible Interpretation. A
Teaching Book.* (San Francisco; Harper & Row, 1988); *What is Midrash?*
(Philadelphia: Fortress Press, 1987); *A Midrash Reader* (Minneapolis:
Augsburg-Fortress, 1990); and *The Midrash: An Introduction* (North-
vale, N.J.: Jason Aronson, 1990). My scholarly work in this area is not
relevant here.

1

The Passionate Love Affair of God and Israel

The sages who compiled Song of Songs Rabbah read the Song of Songs as a sequence of statements of urgent love between God and Israel, the holy people. How they convey the intensity of their—Israel's—love of God forms the point of special interest in this document, for it is not in propositions that they choose to speak but in the medium of symbols. They set forth sequences of words that connote meanings, elicit emotions, stand for events, form the verbal equivalent of pictures, music, dance, or poetry. And through the repertoire of these verbal symbols and their arrangement and rearrangement, the message our authors wish to convey emerges: not in so many words, but through words nonetheless. That is why this remarkable document provides the single best entry in all canonical literature of Judaism into the symbolic system and structure of the Judaism of the dual Torah. Our sages have chosen for their compilation appeal to a highly restricted list of implicit meanings, calling upon some very few events or persons, repeatedly identifying these as the expressions of God's profound affection for Israel and Israel's deep love for God. The message of the document comes not so much from stories of what happened or did not happen, assertions of truth or denials of error, but rather from the repetitious, yet never boring, rehearsal of sets of symbols.

To understand the setting in which our sages read this love poetry, we turn to the Mishnah's treatment of it. The passage is at Mishnah-tractate Yadayyim 3:5. The issue is which documents are regarded as holy among the received canon of ancient Israel. The specific problem focuses upon Qohelet (Ecclesiastes) and the Song of Songs. The terms of the issue derive from the matter of uncleanness. For our purpose, it suffices to know that if a document is holy, then it is held to be unclean, meaning, if one touches that document, one has to undergo a process of purification before eating food in a certain status of sanctification (the details are unimportant here) or, when the Temple stood, go to the Temple. What that meant in practice was that people would be quite cautious about handling such documents which then would be regarded as subject to special protection. So when sages declared that a parchment or hide on which certain words were written imparted uncleanness to hands, they mean to say, those words and the object on which they are written must be handled reverently and thoughtfully.

Now in this context, the issue is, are Qohelet and Song of Songs holy in the way in which the Pentateuch and the Prophets are holy? Here is the passage:

> All sacred scriptures impart uncleanness to hands. The Song of Songs and Qohelet impart uncleanness to hands.
>
> Rabbi Judah says, "Song of Songs imparts uncleanness to hands, but as to Qohelet there is dispute."
>
> Rabbi Yose says, "Qohelet does not impart uncleanness to hands, but as to Song of Songs there is dispute."
>
> Rabbi Simeon says, "Qohelet is among the lenient rulings of the House of Shammai and strict rulings of the House of Hillel."
>
> Said Rabbi Simeon ben Azzai, "I have a tradition from the testimony of the seventy-two elders, on the day on which they seated Rabbi Eleazar ben Azariah in the session, that the Song of Songs and Qohelet do impart uncleanness to hands."

> Said Rabbi Aqiba, "Heaven forbid! No Israelite man ever disputed concerning Song of Songs that it imparts uncleanness to hands. For the entire age is not so worthy as the day on which the Song of Songs was given to Israel. For all the scriptures are holy, but the Song of Songs is holiest of all.' And if they disputed, they disputed only concerning Qohelet."
>
> Said Rabbi Yohanan ben Joshua the son of Rabbi Aqiba's father-in-law, according to the words of Ben Azzai, "Indeed did they dispute, and indeed did they come to a decision."

Clearly, the Mishnah-passage (ca. 200 C.E.) records a point at which the status of the Song of Songs is in doubt. But by the time of the compilation of Song of Songs Rabbah, that question had been settled. Everybody took for granted that our document was holy, and in these pages, we see how that premise yielded a coherent reading of it.

In reading the love songs of the Song of Songs as the story of the love affair of God and Israel, our sages identify implicit meanings that are always few and invariably self-evident. No serious effort goes into demonstrating the fact that God speaks, or Israel speaks; the point of departure is the message and meaning the One or the other means to convey. To take one instance, time and again we shall be told that a certain expression of love in the poetry of the Song of Songs is God's speaking to Israel about (1) the Sea, (2) Sinai, and (3) the world to come; or (1) the first redemption, the one from Egypt; (2) the second redemption, the one from Babylonia; and (3) the third redemption, the one at the end of days. The repertoire of symbols covers Temple and schoolhouse, personal piety and public worship, and other matched pairs and sequences of coherent matters, all of them seen as embedded within the poetry. Here is scripture's poetry read as metaphor, and the task of the reader is to know for which each image of the poem stands. So Israel's holy life is metaphorized through the poetry of love and beloved, Lover and Israel. When African Americans read Exodus as the story of their journey from slavery to freedom, when Jewish Americans read Isaiah 53 as the story of the Holocaust, to take two readily accessible examples, we understand how Scripture serves as a metaphor for our lives, and that is how God speaks to us, through a personal letter, this morning, in the words of scripture.

This highly restricted vocabulary—some might call it a symbolic vocabulary in that messages are conveyed not through propositions but through visual or verbal images—shows us that scripture supplied a highly restricted vocabulary. Meanings were few and to be repeated, not many and to be cast aside promiscuously. We do not find endless multiple meanings[1] but a highly limited repertoire of a few cogent and wholly coherent meanings to be replayed again and again. It is the repetitious character of discourse, in which people say the same thing in a great many different ways, that characterizes this document. The treatment of the Song of Songs by our sages of blessed memory who compiled Song of Songs Rabbah shows over and over again that long lists of alternative meanings or interpretations end up saying just one thing, but in different ways. The implicit meanings prove very few indeed. And that is as it should be, because God says only some few things, but with enormous effect: "Love your neighbor as yourself," for instance, or "Love the Lord your God with all your heart, with all your soul, and with all your might."

Not only so, but I maintain, in Song of Songs Rabbah, the repertoire of meanings is provoked by the Song of Songs itself, its power and its appeal. No one can read the Song of Songs without seeing the poetry as analogy for the love he or she holds most dear. Here we see how deeply and unreservedly our sages loved Israel and loved God, and so found self-evident the messages of the Song of Songs that supplied metaphors for that love. In this way I mean to show the opportunity that the sages of Judaism recognized and emphasize the magnificence of their theological achievement.

How does speech through verbal symbols take place in our document? It is through setting forth lists of items, different from one another, that in response to a given verse of Song of Songs form a single category, namely, illustrations of the sentiment of said verse. When in Song of Songs Rabbah there is a sequence of items alleged to form taxon, that is, a set of things that share a common taxic indicator, what we have is a list. The list presents diverse matters that all share together and therefore also set forth a single fact or rule or phenomenon. That is why we can list them, in all their distinctive character and specificity, in a common catalogue of "other things" that pertain all together to one thing. And, in our minds, when we see things combined in a list that we had not thought subject to combination, that is the point at which the Song of Songs makes its impact: this verse is illustrated by these (familiar) items. In the surprising juxtaposition of things we had not imagined comparable to one another, a metaphor is formed—one to which, as in the metaphors of poetry, music, dance, or visual art, we respond in other than verbal ways.

What is set on display justifies the display: putting this familiar fact together with that familiar fact in an unfamiliar combination constitutes what is new and important in the list; the consequent conclusion one is supposed to draw, the proposition or rule that emerges—these are rarely articulated (my list of propositional composites shows the possibility) and never important. What we have is a kind of subtle restatement through an infinite range of possibilities of the combinations and recombinations of a few essentially simple facts (data). It is as though a magician tossed a set of sticks this way and that, interpreting the diverse combinations of a fixed set of objects. The propositions that emerge are not the main point. The combinations are.

The technical language that we shall see again and again in the formation of lists is, "another matter," in Hebrew, *davar aher*. The davar-aher construction plays on what theological "things"— names, places, events, actions are deemed to bear theological weight and to affect attitude and action. The play is worked out by a reprise of available materials which are composed in some fresh and interesting combination. When three or more such theological things are combined, they form a theological structure, and, viewed all together, all of the theological things in a given document constitute the components of the entire theological structure that the document affords. The propostions portrayed visually through metaphors of sight, dramatically through metaphors of action and relationship, or in attitude and emotion through metaphors that convey or provoke feeling and sentiment, prove familiar and commonplace when translated into language. The work of the theologian in this context is not to say something new or even persuasive, for the former is unthinkable by definition, the latter unnecessary in context. It is rather to display theological things in a fresh and interesting way, to accomplish a fresh exegesis of the canon of theological things.

To take one example, what do the compilers say through their readings of the metaphor of the nut tree for Israel? First, Israel prospers when it gives scarce resources for the study of the Torah or for carrying out religious duties; second, Israel sins but atones,

and Torah is the medium of atonement; third, Israel is identified through carrying out its religious duties, e.g., circumcision;
fourth, Israel's leaders must be cautious; fifth, Israel may be nothing now but will experience a glorious time in the coming age;
sixth, Israel has plenty of room for outsiders but cannot afford to
lose a single one of its number. What we have is a repertoire of
fundamentals, dealing with Torah and Torah study, the moral life
and atonement, Israel and its holy way of life, and Israel and its
coming salvation. Nothing is left out.

Do these propositions correspond in their way to any of the
composites of figures, events, actions, and the like of which our
davar-aher composites are composed? A survey of these composites shows the contradictory facts that they are heterogeneous but
their components derive from a limited list of scriptural events
and personalities on the one side and virtues of the Torah's holy
way of life on the other. Here is a survey:

Joseph, righteous men, Moses, and Solomon;
patriarchs as against princes, offerings as against merit, and
Israel as against the nations; those who love the king, proselytes, martyrs, penitents;
first, Israel at Sinai; then Israel's loss of God's presence on
account of the golden calf; then God's favoring Israel by
treating Israel not in accord with the requirements of justice
but with mercy;
Dathan and Abiram, the spies, Jeroboam, Solomon's marriage
to Pharaoh's daughter, Ahab, Jezebel, Zedekiah;
Israel is feminine, the enemy (Egypt) masculine, but God the
father saves Israel the daughter;
Moses and Aaron, the Sanhedrin, the teachers of scripture and
Mishnah, the rabbis;
the disciples, the relationship among disciples, public recitation of teachings of the Torah in the right order; lections of
the Torah;
the spoil at the sea = the Exodus, the Torah, the Tabernacle,
the ark;
the patriarchs, Abraham, Isaac, Jacob, then Israel in Egypt, Israel's atonement and God's forgiveness;
the Temple where God and Israel are joined, the Temple as
God's resting place, the Temple as the source of Israel's
fecundity;

Israel in Egypt, at the sea, at Sinai, and subjugated by the gentile kingdoms, and how the redemption will come;

Rebecca, those who came forth from Egypt, Israel at Sinai, acts of loving-kingness, the kingdoms that now rule Israel, the coming redemption;

fire above, fire below, meaning heavenly and altar fires; Torah in writing, Torah in memory; fire of Abraham, Moriah, bush, Elijah, Hananiah, Mishael, and Azariah;

the Ten Commandments, show-fringes and phylacteries, recitation of the Shema and the Prayer, the tabernacle and the cloud of the presence of God, and the mezuzah;

the timing of redemption, the moral condition of those to be redeemed, and the past religious misdeeds of those to be redeemed;

Israel at the sea, Sinai, the Ten Commandments; then the synagogues and school houses; then the redeemer;

the Exodus, the conquest of the land of Israel, the redemption and restoration of Israel to Zion after the destruction of the first Temple, and the final and ultimate salvation;

the Egyptians, Esau and his generals, and, finally, the four kingdoms;

Moses' redemption, the first, to the second redemption in the time of the Babylonians and Daniel;

the litter of Solomon: the priestly blessing, the priestly watches, the Sanhedrin, and the Israelites coming out of Egypt;

Israel at the sea and forgiveness for sins effected through their passing through the sea, Israel at Sinai, the war with Midian, the crossing of the Jordan and entry into the land of Israel, the house of the sanctuary, the priestly watches, the offerings in the Temple, the Sanhedrin, the Day of Atonement;

God redeemed Israel without preparation; the nations of the world will be punished after Israel is punished; the nations of the world will present Israel as gifts to the royal messiah, and here the base-verse refers to Abraham, Isaac, Jacob, Sihon, Og, Canaanites;

the return to Zion in the time of Ezra, the Exodus from Egypt in the time of Moses;

the patriarchs and with Israel in Egypt, at the sea, and then before Sinai;

Abraham, Jacob, Moses;

Isaac, Jacob, Esau, Jacob, Joseph, the brothers, Jonathan, David, Saul, man, wife, paramour;

Abraham in the fiery furnace and Shadrach, Meshach, and Abednego, the exile in Babylonia, now with reference to the return to Zion

and so forth.

These components form not a theological system, made up of well-joined propositions and harmonious positions, nor do I discern in the several lists propositions that I can specify and that are demonstrated syllogistically through comparison and contrast. The point is just the opposite; it is to show that many different things really do belong on the same list. That yields not a proposition that the list syllogistically demonstrates. The list yields only itself—but then the list invites our exegesis; the connections among these items require exegesis (of course, that is, eisegesis). What this adds up to, then, is not argument for proposition, hence comparison and contrast and rule making of a philosophical order, but rather a theological structure—comprising well-defined attitudes. Somewhere on the path from emotion to attitude to proposition, Song of Songs Rabbah takes up its position, sometimes here, sometimes there, but never in one place for long.

What is important in the davar-aher constructions is not the proposition but the interesting array and arrangement of the components themselves. That is why I have insisted that the davar-aher construction serves without consequential propositional result, even though it very commonly yields some sort of commonplace affirmation. But the details, where the framers have put their best work, serve to repeat in many ways that one point, commonly, the right attitude; in the Mishnah's counterpart, the details serve to demonstrate a proposition. The difference then seems to be that the Mishnah's list contributes toward a system, while Song of Songs Rabbah's list portrays a structure. The theological purpose therefore is to arrange and rearrange a few simple propositions represented by a limited vocabulary of symbols. In such a structure we organize set piece tableaus, rather than putting forth and demonstrating propositions. Philosophy's sylogistic argument on behalf of well-tested propositions contrasts with theology's evocation through well-arrayed symbols of correct attitudes.

In a word, we find in the davar-aher construction a selection, that is, a canon of things that pertain to theology, chosen out of a larger but still highly restricted canon of candidates, all serving, each in itself, all in various combinations and recombinations, a single purpose: to portray in many ways in a systematic and orderly manner, the representation of God's relationship to Israel. The relationship is one of love, and that is always the same; but it is a relationship of many splendors, captured, after all, in all those aspects and objects that contain and express and convey the love: whether the Torah and its study, whether Moses and David, whether the "event"[2] at the sea and at Sinai. To identify that canon—the theological things on the list, the source of those things, the way in which those things combine and recombine to form a cogent portrait—we consult the combinations and recombinations defined for us by our document. Then the davar-aher construction forms a theological structure within a larger theological structure: a reworking of canonical materials. We see how these verbal symbols, irreducible minima, are worked and reworked, rethought and recast in some other way or order or combination—but always held to be the same thing throughout. The possibilities out of which our authorship has made its selections are limited not by the metaphorical potential of the Song of Songs but by the contents of the Hebrew scriptures.

For every Abraham, Isaac, and Jacob that we find, there are Job, Enoch, Jeroboam, or Zephaniah, whom we do not find; for every sea/Sinai/entry into the land of Israel that we do find, there are other sequences, e.g., the loss of the ark to the Philistines and its recovery, or Barak and Deborah, that we do not find. Granted, Sinai must enjoy a privileged position throughout. But why prefer Shadrach, Meshach, and Abednego or Hananiah, Mishael, and Azariah over other trilogies of heroic figures? So the selection is an act. But once restricted, the same selected theological things then undergo combination and recombination with other theological things.

Out of Song of Songs Rabbah we may undertake the description of the theological structure and system of the Judaism of the dual Torah. By theological description I mean the account of the principles and ideas concerning God's relationship with Israel (for we speak of a Judaism) that form the foundation and substrate of the thought that comes to expression in a variety of canonical writings. The problem has been the character of the documents and their mode of theological discourse. They are not Greek philosophers with the gift of generalizing their thought in abstract language. They are philosophers with other gifts altogether: with the power to speak in concrete language about abstract things. That explains why the philosophical character of some of the important classical writings of Judaism has been ignored or simply missed by people used to a more conventional kind of writing.

It is not that the writers speak only in concrete terms; we could readily move from their detail to our abstraction and speak in general terms about the coherence of prevailing principles of a theological order. The problem has been much more profound. We face a set of writings that clearly mean to tell us about God and God's relationship to Israel, and about Israel and Israel's relationship to God. The authorships a priori exhibit the conviction that the thoughts of the whole are cogent and coherent, since they prove deeply concerned with identifying contradiction, disharmony, and incoherence and removing it. But we have not known how to find the connections between what they have written and the structure or system of thought that leads them to say, in detail, the things that they say.

When we propose to describe the theological system to which a piece of well-crafted writing testifies, our task is easy when, to begin with, the writing discusses in syllogistic logic and within an appropriate program of propositions what we conceive to be theological themes or problems. Hence, it is generally conceded, we may legitimately translate the topically theological writings of Paul, Augustine, or Luther into the systematic and coherent theologies of those three figures, respectively: finding order and structure in materials of a cogent theological character. But what about the literature that to begin with does not set forth theological propositions in philosophical form, even while using profoundly religious language for self-evidently religious purposes? Surely that literature testifies to an orderly structure or system of thought, for the alternative is to impute to the contents of those writings the status of mere episodic and unsystematic observations about this and that. True, profound expressions of piety may exhibit the traits of intellectual chaos and disorder, and holy simplicity may mask confusion.

But, as I have already stressed, such a description of the rabbinic literature of late antiquity, which I call the canon of the Judaism of the dual Torah, defies the most definitive and indicative traits of the writings. These are order, system, cogency, coherence, proportion, and fine and well-crafted thought. The compilers of Song of Songs Rabbah proposed to say one thing in a great many ways. So, by their own character, these writings point toward some sort of logic and order and structure that as a matter of fact finds attestation in the writings themselves. And when we seek to articulate the principles of order and structure as these pertain to the fundamental characteristics of God, the Torah, and Israel, we set forth the theology of the canon of the Judaism of the dual Torah.

Now that simple and everywhere-acknowledged fact of the yearning for order and structure characteristic of that Judaism leads us to the question of these essays: How to move from literature to the description of a theological system that gives sense, structure, and cogency to the literature's fundamental convictions? What is the theology, or what are the theologies, that makes the literature what it is: coherent in sense and in meaning? That is the question that faces anyone who wants to know whether the canonical literature of the Judaism of the dual Torah constitutes a mass of discrete observations about this and that or a well-crafted structure and system. For the canonical writings, appealing to God's revelation to Moses at Sinai, everywhere calling upon God and spelling out what God wants of Israel in quest of God and God's service, form one of the great religious writings of humanity. But do these writings yield theology, in addition to religion? That is to say, can we seen them as system, structure, order, and not merely as a vast and confusing mass of half-coherent thoughts? And how are we to test the perception of order amid the appearance of chaos, such as these writings create?

To begin with, we have to justify the theological inquiry into literature that self-evidently does not conform to the conventions of theological discourse to which Western civilization in its Greco-Roman heritage and Christian (and, as a matter of fact, Muslim) civilization in its philosophical formulation has made us accustomed. The Muslim and Christian theological heritage, formulated within the conventions of philosophical argument, joined by a much smaller (and generally neglected) Judaic theological corpus, to be sure, does not allow us to read as a theological statement a single canonical writing of the Judaism of the dual Torah of late antiquity. So if the literary canons of Western theology are to govern, then, by definition, the literature of Judaism in its formative age can present no theological order or system.

That proposition hardly proves compelling. For it is difficult for us to imagine a mental universe so lacking in structure, form, and order as to permit everything and its opposite to be said about God, to imagine a God so confused and self-contradictory as to yield a truly unintelligible relevation lacking all cogency.[3] The very premises of all theology—that there is order, structure, and composition, proportion, and form, in God's mind, which in fact is intelligible to us through the medium of relevation properly construed—a priori render improbable the hypothesis that the canonical writings of the Judaism of the dual Torah violate every rule of intelligible discourse concerning the principal and foundation of all being. If, after all, we really cannot speak intelligibly about God, the Torah, holy Israel, and what God wants of us, then why write all those books to begin with?

The character of the literature, its rather hermetic modes of discourse, arcane language of thought, insistence upon speaking only about detail and rarely about the main point—these traits of discourse stand in the way of description of theology because of their very unsyllogistic character. And yet, if we consider not the received modes of discourse of theology in our civilization but rather the problem and topic of theology—systematic and orderly thinking about God through the medium of revelation— we can hardly find a more substantial or suitable corpus of writing for theological analysis than the literature of the Judaism of the dual Torah. At the end of our inquiry, we shall reflect on how the dual Torah that is Judaism makes its theological statement.

Notes

1. Cf. William Scott Green, "Romancing the Tome: Rabbinic Hermeneutics and the Theory of Literature," *Semeia* (1987) 40: 147–69, = *Text and Textuality,* ed. Charles Winquist, with special reference to p. 163: "If it is doubtful that rabbis ascribed 'endless multiple meanings' to scripture, it is no less so that rabbinic hermeneutics encourages and routinely tolerated the metonymical coexistence of different meanings of scripture that did not, and could not, annul one another."

2. I put "event" into quotation marks, because in this context, that word cannot possibly mean what it means in ordinary and secular contexts. This event is not a singular happening and it also is not a paradigm—not singular because it defines, not paradigmatic because it is always, in the end, particular to itself and its own details. It is not meant to be spiritualized but meant always to govern.

3. As a matter of fact, the great Zoroastrian theologians of the ninth century criticized Judaism (and other religions) on just this point (see "Zoroastrian Critique of Judaism," in my *History of the Jews in Babylonia* [Leiden: E. J. Brill, 1969], 4: 403–23). Not a single Judaic thinker, however—whether a philosopher or a theologian, whether in the Islamic or the Western theological/philosophical tradition—has ever entertained the proposition that the God who gave the Torah is confused and arbitrary. Why should anyone have thought so, when, after all, the entire dynamic of Judaic thought embodied within the halakhic tradition from the Yerushalmi and Bavli forward has aimed at the systematization, harmonization, and ordering of confusing but never confused, facts of the Torah. There is, therefore, no possibility of finding in the Judaism of the dual Torah the slightest hint of an unsystematic system, an atheological corpus of thought.

2

Song of Songs Rabbah
to Song of Songs 1:2

O that you would kiss me with the
kisses of your mouth!
For your love is better than wine.

Our first encounter with Song of Songs Rabbah carries us to a
large and complex chapter. We address the entire chapter, so as to
find out how the writers of the book have done their work. In
subsequent chapters we shall focus upon what is said, understanding how the message is delivered, of what it is comprised,
and why it takes the form it does rather than some other. We have
the opportunity here to see how the document's compilers do
their work on a large scale, so to begin with we shall focus upon
the structure and organization of the whole. To be sure, we are
interested not only in how our authors make their statement, but
also what they wish to say. Once we know the how, we shall find
the discovery of the what easy. We shall pay a great deal of attention to the rather run-on quality of the whole, and I shall try to
show you that the chapter before us, and therefore the document
as a whole, is crafted with great care and a clear sense of coherence and proportion. Since the evidence that will strike your
eye will give you the opposite impression, and you will see the

chapter as somewhat disorganized, run-on, a sequence of this, that, and the other thing that happens to pop into someone's mind, my task will not be an easy one. But once you grasp what is happening, you will find little difficulty in making sense of how the framers have organized any chapter of this Midrash-compilation or a great many others. So it is worth the effort at the outset to ask questions of organization and presentation. Along the way, of course, we shall pay close attention to what is said, but the translation itself ought to convey the propositions of the various compositions and the coherence of the several composites as well.

The first fact that strikes us as we begin our work is simple. The Song of Songs is not read whole and complete, or even in large units. It is read phrase by phrase, or, at most, verse by verse. So the historical or original intent of the poet/author is set aside, and his work is dismantled and recomposed in its smallest parts. In that way, the received poem is taken out of its initial context, which is treated as inconsequential; the new context is defined, as we shall see, in other terms altogether. And yet, if we were to conclude, the Song of Songs is now going to be treated as a mere pretext, allowing our sages to say anything they want without regard to the common sense of the text at hand, we would err. For, as we shall see, our sages pay very close attention to the sense of the clause or verse they address. Song of Songs speaks of love. Our sages do too. The Song speaks of kisses and caresses. Our sages do too. But for our sages, the starting point of all love is love of God for Israel, love of Israel for God, and from there, their work commences. What they want to know is where in the record of revelation God and Israel caress one another, and that question is raised at the very outset.

The second fact that we must observe follows from the first. Our document is organized around the verses of the Song of Songs, read in order. Song of Songs is the trellis, and our Midrash-comments the vines. While we dismantle the Song, we also highlight its prominence as the organizing principle in all that we shall say. Since the verses, in sequence, govern throughout, I call the verse subject to discussion (whether it is the text that is analyzed or the pretext for what the framer wishes to say anyhow) the base-verse, in that it defines the foundation of discourse. In our opening discussion, that base-verse is amplified. We want to know who is speaking, on what occasion, and to whom. That question compels attention, since, Song of Songs never appears to speak of God, and what the Song does describe on the surface hardly is a sacred relationship. But, of course, the opposite is the case, so every figure in our document—the named sages and also the voice of the document itself—will take as premise and fact throughout the conception that the love here is God's for Israel.

II:i.1   A. "O that you would kiss me with the kisses of your mouth! [For your love is better than wine]":

          B. In what connection was this statement made?

We start the passage with a citation of a clause of a verse, and, as we shall see, that always sets the limits of discussion. Rarely do we consider two verses together and never more than that. So, as we see, the question we ask is defined by the smallest whole sense-unit of the scriptural passage. Where does Israel speak to God in these terms? The answer is at C and D.

          C. Rabbi Hinena ben Rabbi Pappa said, "It was stated at the sea: '[I compare you, my love] to a mare of Pharaoh's chariots' " (Song 1:9).

          D. Rabbi Judah ben Rabbi Simon said, "It was stated at Sinai: 'The song of songs' (Song 1:1)—the song that was sung by the singers: 'The singers go before, the minstrels follow after' " (Ps. 68:26).

The statement, "O that you would kiss me with the kisses of your mouth" speaks for Israel at the sea, where Israel speaks of its love of God, or it is a song sung in the Temple (see Ps. 68:26). The single striking point here and throughout is that most of the statements are joined to verses of scripture in other passages altogether. Citation of other passages of scripture means that the entire repertoire of Israel's history—that is, its life with God told in the form of narrative—contributes to the reading of any one clause. All issues of order and sequence are set aside. Israel's history forms a vast tableau, available for the task of illustrating our verse. So on the one side, we dismantle our text into its bits and pieces. On the other, we do the same with the whole record of scripture. Then we reconstitute the one in the context of the other.

Does that mean we can say just about anything we want? In theory, the answer is yes; in practice, no. Once we dismantle a set of texts and look at each phrase of each text out of documentary context, we can more or less say whatever we want. It is as though we turned the writings of Shakespeare into a mere dictionary or word list. We could then write the front page of this morning's newspaper out of Shakespeare, making provision, of course, for some anachronisms. But then we have lost Shakespeare to produce a merely archaic form of journalistic writing. And that is not what happens here. The reason, as we already know, is that the premise of all reading of the Song of Songs is that it expresses the story of love: Israel's and God's, together and reciprocally. So we have to read each phrase of the Song in light of all *relevant* moments in Israel's life, such as other passages of scripture set forth. Not every moment in Israel's life is relevant to "kiss me with kisses of his mouth," but only those moments at which God speaks in terms of love to Israel, or vice versa. And Hinena finds just such a verse, where God says of Israel, "I compare you, my love. . . ."

Judah's statement stands alongside, but in fact does not intersect with Hinena's. He is referring to a different clause, namely, "the song of songs," and what he wants to know is where this truly distinctive song ("the song of songs" implies the classic, the best, the model) was sung. It was, of course, said at Sinai: Sinai is the climax of the love, the point at which God took over Israel and spread over Israel the cloak of his love.

Had the framer who set these two statements side by side made a mistake? Obviously not, since the upshot of the two separate statements is the same. Both speak of moments of true communion, one at the miracle at the sea, the other at Sinai; and the one means nothing without the other. God's love for Israel at the sea opened the way to the consummation of that love at Sinai. The two statements singly prove incomplete; together they tell the whole story. We are going to hear the words "at the sea," and "Sinai," time and again. They will never be spelled out and no propositions will be attached to them. But they always will evoke a clear and present sentiment: a picture that serves for a thousand words. Say "sea" in this document, say "Sinai" here—and you need say no more.

It suffices to note, also, that we know nothing more about Judah and Hinena than their names. We shall not be told anything about the authorities in our writing other than that they stand behind a statement. These names are introduced not because we care who the people are, when they made their statements, or why they said them (for instance, as part of some larger theology they were working out). On the contrary, just as we work with phrases, so we work with anonymous figures, bearing names but little more than that. Matching phrase to phrase, placing a named authority with the combination—all of this creates the effect of a new order of things. Scripture is recast, its original lines of structure obscured; new figures that are not in scripture at all take up a position in relationship to the recombinancy of verses or clauses of scripture. Scripture flows into the Torah, the written now formed into a component of the whole Torah, oral and written; and sages—the Judahs and Hinenas and other named but profoundly anonymous figures in the great chain of tradition from Sinai—guide the current.

And yet—and yet who speaks to us? Let's take another look at the passage, now whole and complete:

II:i.1   A. "O that you would kiss me with the kisses of your mouth! [For your love is better than wine]":
          B. In what connection was this statement made?
          C. Rabbi Hinena ben Rabbi Pappa said, "It was stated at the sea: '[I compare you, my love] to a mare of Pharaoh's chariots'" (Song 1:9).
          D. Rabbi Judah ben Rabbi Simon said, "It was stated at Sinai: 'The song of songs' (Song 1:1)—the song that was sung by the singers: 'The singers go before, the minstrels follow after'" (Ps. 68:26).

As soon as we see the passage whole, we realize that it is made up of three free-standing sentences, A, C, and D. By themselves, C and D refer back to A—but only through the intervention of

B. In what connection was this statement made? Without that
question, the composition falls apart into unrelated sentences. C
without A is senseless, and D may stand entirely autonomous of
A, and all the more so of C. It is B that forms the whole into a cogent statement, one that can say what it says here and nothing
else. Then who says B? No named party, but the voice of the document, or the author of this composition, small but perfect and
beyond the possibility of change. We may dismantle the Song of
Songs and find meanings in the parts. We may not dismantle this
little set of four sentences and still make sense of the parts. That is
what I mean when I say, "one can say what it says here and nothing else."

Who speaks here speaks throughout: the voice is the voice of
the document. When rabbis preach sermons and cite Midrash-
passages, as they often do, they will say simply, "the Midrash
says . . ." or "the Talmud says . . ." While a labor-saving device,
making it unnecessary to refer to sense in context, this personifi-
cation of the writing corresponds in a deep way to the character
of the contents. The document holds together a vast corpus of
references, allusions, citations, and, in the end, outside the frame-
work of the document as a whole, all of these references and
allusions and citations fall to pieces and lose all determinate
meaning. So the framer of the document, or, here, the author of
the little composition and the one who formed of this composition and of others a composite that all together made a coherent
statement—these are, in the end, that voice, the one who speaks
through B, on the one side, but through the entire formation of
A–D, on the other. Now if you want to call the author of the
composition or the compositor who has gathered a number of
compositions "the voice of the document," you are justified in
doing so. But in the theological language of Judaism, the right
name for these writers is simply, "the Midrash says" or "the
Talmud says," and the truly appropriate name is simply: "the
Torah says."

When I spoke of writing with scripture, one of the things that
I meant was as follows: scripture forms the vocabulary of a language, contributing words and phrases ("Sinai," "the sea"), but
scripture also defines the syntax and grammar of the language,
contributing principles of intelligibility ("God loves Israel, Israel
loves God"). Hence, out of words and phrases, we are permitted
to say some things but not other things. And that is why we could

debate whether or not Song of Songs "imparts uncleanness to hands," meaning, enters the Torah. Does it violate the rules of syntax and grammar? In context, that means, it says what cannot be said. Then it is not a holy book; God does not speak here, because this book contradicts what God says in other holy books. But again and again we now demonstrate the contrary. God's messages are here, as much as elsewhere. How do we know? Because we hear "the sea," "Sinai" just as much as we hear those words, that message elsewhere.

To understand the compositions that follow, Nos. 2–6, we have to remember that the compositors of our document propose a long string of answers to a single question. What we have is a set of such answers, each standing on its own, as much as Judah's and Hinena's statements stand on their own. But all of the statements are reworked to take account of the program of the compositors. We know that fact because at each point, the original question, "In what connection was this statement made?" is answered, but never repeated.

The expression of love now comes from the Holy One, blessed be he, the ministering angels, on the occasion of the tent of meeting, on the occasion of the "eternal house" or "house of the ages," that is to say, the holy Temple in Jerusalem where God was served through the offerings described in the books of Leviticus and Numbers. If we put all this together we get two distinct portraits: one of God or the ministering angels speaking; the other, the occasion or location at which the statement (in this case, the Song as a whole) was made. Is there a conclusion to be drawn? No proposition is announced, just a sequence of what we might now call "word-bytes," that is, words that conjur visions. Then the visions are those of (1) where: the sea, Sinai; (2) who: God or the angels speaking to Israel; (3) why: the tabernacle in the wilderness, the Temple in Jerusalem. And what is the message? A variety of propositions will serve to correspond to these symbols in verbal form. The power of the composite emerges when you try to list all of the messages: all are right; all are pertinent; none exhausts the possibilities of the tableau.

2   A. It was taught on Tannaite authority in the name of Rabbi Nathan, "The Holy One, blessed be he, in the glory of his greatness said it: 'The song of songs that is Solomon's'" (Song 1:1),

    B. "[meaning,] that belongs to the King to whom peace belongs." [The Hebrew name, Solomon, in Hebrew, is formed of the word for peace, shalom—Shelomo. The ending, *-o,* means, his. Thus: the king to whom peace belongs.]

3   A. Rabban Gamaliel says, "The ministering angels said it: 'the song of songs'" (Song 1:1)—

    B. "the song that the princes on high said."

4   A. Rabbi Yohanan said, "It was said at Sinai: 'O that you would kiss me with the kisses of your mouth!'" (Song 1:2)

5   A. Rabbi Meir says, "It was said in connection with the tent of meeting."

What follows requires a word of clarification. B–H do not advance the discussion we have had up to this point, and they interrupt the progression to No. 6, which continues the established form and program. In fact the set of sentences is inserted to clarify and justify Meir's position. A different verse altogether is adduced in evidence, and each of the elements of that verse is identified with offerings in the Temple or tent of meeting. Meir holds that these offerings were presented in the tent of meeting in the wilderness, and that fact sustains his position. The intrusion is somewhat jarring for us, of course. The reason is that, in good writing, material that interrupts the main point, for instance, references or buttressing information not required to advance an argument but only to support it, go into footnotes.

Why no footnotes to assist our reading? The answer, of course, is that, in ancient times, when there was no printing but only copying, a text was represented in long columns of undifferentiated words, with little punctuation and few markers of beginning, middle, or ending, paragraphs, chapters, or the like. Consequently, writers had no choice but to include in the body of the text everything that they wished to say. That is why our document, among many rabbinic writings, gives the impression of a somewhat meandering and slightly out-of-focus statement, with this, that, and the other thing thrown in to impede our progress from point to point. Once we visually identify footnote material, we see how exquisitely orderly and carefully crafted this document, among all rabbinic writings of ancient times, really is.

> B. And he brings evidence from the following verse: "Awake, O north wind, and come, O south wind! Blow upon my garden, let its fragrance be wafted abroad. Let my beloved come to his garden, and eat its choicest fruits" (Song 4:16).
>
> C. "Awake, O north wind": this refers to the burnt offerings, which were slaughtered at the north side of the altar.
>
> D. "and come, O south wind": this refers to the peace offerings, which were slaughtered at the south side of the altar.
>
> E. "Blow upon my garden": this refers to the tent of meeting.
>
> F. "let its fragrance by wafted abroad": this refers to the incense offering.
>
> G. "Let my beloved come to his garden": this refers to the presence of God.
>
> H. "and eat its choicest fruits": this refers to the offerings.

The inserted materials are themselves cogent: clause plus paraphrase, time after time; and the sense and intent of the whole leave no doubt on the proposition that is demonstrated.

> 6   A. Rabbis say, "It was said in connection with the house of the ages [the Temple itself]."
>
> B. And they bring evidence from the same verse: "Awake, O north wind, and come, O south wind! Blow upon my garden, let its fragrance be wafted abroad. Let my beloved come to his garden, and eat its choicest fruits" (Song 4:16).
>
> C. "Awake, O north wind": this refers to the burnt offerings, which are slaughtered at the north side of the altar.
>
> D. "and come, O south wind": this refers to the peace offerings, which were slaughtered at the south side of the altar.

E. "Blow upon my garden": this refers to the house of the ages.

F. "let its fragrance be wafted abroad": this refers to the incense offering.

G. "Let my beloved come to his garden": this refers to the presence of God.

H. "and eat its choicest fruits": this refers to the offerings.

I. The rabbis furthermore maintain that all the other verses also refer to the house of the ages.

J. Said Rabbi Aha, "The verse that refers to the Temple is the following: 'King Solomon made himself a palanquin, from the wood of Lebanon. He made its posts of silver, its back of gold, its seat of purple; it was lovingly wrought within by the daughters of Jerusalem' " (Song 3:9–10).

K. Rabbis treat these as the intersecting verses for the verse, 'And it came to pass on the day that Moses had made an end of setting up the tabernacle' "(Num. 7:1).

What we have here is a dispute, with several parties addressing the same proposition. No. 7 concludes this composite with a secondary point. Each party has told us that to which he thinks our base-verse, "O that you would kiss me with the kisses of your mouth! [For your love is better than wine]," refers. So how does each party explain the evidence presented by the other? The interest in a full and fair exposition of all viewpoints underlines the congenial atmosphere of this "dispute." At stake is what God has said in scripture. Argument is fair, because the goal is truth. No party wishes to talk down, belittle, or ridicule the other, and every party proposes to listen carefully to the other: he might be right!

7   A. In the opinion of Rabbi Hinena [1.C], who said that the verse was stated on the occasion of the sea, [the sense of the verse, "O that you would kiss me with the kisses of your mouth"] is, "may he bring to rest upon us the Holy Spirit, so that we may say before him many songs."

B. In the opinion of Rabban Gamaliel, who said that the verse was stated by the ministering angels, [the sense of the verse, "O that you would kiss me with the kisses of your mouth"] is, "may he give us the kisses that he gave to his sons."

C. In the opinion of Rabbi Meir, who said that the verse was stated in connection with the tent of meeting, [the sense of the verse, "O that you would kiss me with the kisses of your mouth"] is, "May he send fire down to us and so accept his offerings."

D. In the opinion of Rabbi Yohanan, who said that the verse was stated in connection with Sinai, [the sense of the verse, "O that you would kiss me with the kisses of your mouth"] is, "May he cause kisses to issue for us from his mouth."

E. "That is why it is written, 'O that you would kiss me with the kisses from your mouth.'"

No. 7 once again shows us that our compilers are first-class editors, since they have assembled quite disparate materials and drawn them together into a cogent statement. But the subject is not our base-verse, and hence the compilers cannot have had in mind the need of a commentary of a verse-by-verse principle of conglomeration and organization. The passage as a whole refers in much more general terms to the Song of Songs, and hardly to Song 1:2 in particular. That is shown by the simple fact that various opinions invoke other verses than the one to which the whole is ultimately assigned. This is a highly sophisticated work of compilation, involving rich editorial intervention. Whoever put it all together bears sole responsibility for the whole. Using whatever materials came to hand—this one's opinion, that one's opinion—the author of the individual compositions, but, more to the point, the compositor of the whole, wrote a coherent and beautifully crafted statement for us. And it is his statement (or their statement—we don't know how many people were involved).

The alternative view should be set forth. Since the cited authorities thrived in various times, from the first and second centuries of the Common Era onward, is it possible that the passage has been formed in a process of tradition? That is to say, to the generative questions, where, when, and why was this verse stated, Meir gave his answer, in the second century. Then, whether in memory or in writing, that circulated for a while; then Yohanan, a hundred years later, added his answer; and so on to the end. That theory of tradition may be called agglutinative, in that the parts were added one by one, and not put together into a single cogent statement at the end. Since we have no reliable information on how any of the rabbinic documents took shape, all we may do is form a judgment based on the character of the writing at hand. One view is that so much evidence of careful editing, balance, order, and proportion points to a single act on the part of someone with a plan for the whole. A process of agglutination is unlikely to yield a piece of writing that is so coherent in form over a period of three of four hundred years. The other view is: why not? Rules for adding to a given document can have been observed over three hundred years as well as over two days of work.

The former hypothesis finds decisive support in the organization of the whole more than in the balance and formal perfection of the parts. We noted earlier the topical order: where, who, why. By definition, that topical order cannot be agglutinative. But it does govern, and considerations of sequence of authorities—earlier sages adding their opinions, then later ones adding theirs—are ignored. The one rule we have the right to invoke for a process of tradition is that earlier authorities appear first, then later authorities are added. Any intervention in that order will upset the process of tradition ("agglutination"). To put it differently, if the governing principle is not the order of authorities of the second and third centuries and beyond, then some organizing hand other than tradition is in charge. That is the hand that said, first we deal with where, then who, then, why, and over the centuries, we shall add the opinions of authorities on one topic or another, as they appear over the horizon. Then the process of agglutination is secondary to the program of a single hand or intelligence. If that is the case, then whether the plan came at the outset or at the end, the result is the same: a single statement utilizing opinions given over time is made all at once. Between the alternatives—a plan up front, imposed for four or five hundred years, or a plan at the end, utilizing the detritus of four or five centuries for a single program at the end—the letter strikes me as far more likely.

We have now given a single view of the base-verse, the view that what is important is to identify who, where, and why. Now we proceed to a different interest in the same base-verse: namely, what is going on here, the event of God's love. The introduction, for reasons readers fully understand, announces davar aher, another interpretation.

II:ii.1 A. Another interpretation of the verse, "O that you would kiss me with the kisses of your mouth!"

B. Said Rabbi Yohanan, "An angel would carry forth the Word [the Ten Commandments] from before the Holy One, blessed be he, word by word, going about to every Israelite and saying to him, 'Do you accept upon yourself the authority of this Word? There are so and so many rules that pertain to it, so and so many penalties that pertain to it, so and so many decrees that pertain to it, and so are the religious duties, the lenient aspects, the stringent aspects, that apply to it. There also is a reward that accrues in connection with it.' "

C. "And the Israelite would say, 'Yes.' "

D. "And the other would go and say to him again, 'Do you accept the divinity of the Holy One, blessed be he.' "

E. "And the Israelite would say, 'Yes, yes.' "

F. "Then he would kiss him on his mouth."

G. "That is in line with this verse: 'To you it has been shown, that you might know' (Dt. 4:25) — that is, by an angel."

H. Rabbis say, "It was the Word itself that made the rounds of the Israelites one by one, saying to each one, 'Do you accept me upon yourself? There are so and so many rules that pertain to me, so and so many penalties that pertain to me, so and so many decrees that pertain to me, and so are the religious duties, the lenient aspects, the stringent aspects, that apply to me. There also is a reward that accrues in connection with me.' "

I. "And the Israelite would say, 'Yes.' "

> J. "So he taught him the Torah."
>
> K. "That is in line with this verse: 'Lest you forget the things your eyes saw (Dt. 4:0)'—how the Word spoke with you."

Earlier, the view that the verse was spoken at Sinai is attributed to Yohanan. Now we have an amplification of that view. Both Yohanan and "rabbis," that is, the unnamed majority who dictate the final decision, concur that the verse refers to Sinai. The angel, or God's word itself, kissed the Israelites' mouth, for those mouths said, "Yes, yes," to God's invitation to love contained in the Torah. The issue is a detail. The fact is, God's love is shown at Sinai, that is, in the Torah. We cannot find surprising the fact that a set of footnotes, and footnotes to footnotes, follows. I indent these as before, so that the relationship to the whole will become clear.

> 2 A. Another explanation of the phrase, "Lest you forget the things your eyes saw" (Dt. 4:9):
>
> B. The Israelites heard two acts of speech from the mouth of the Holy One, blessed be he.
>
> 3 A. [Reverting to No. 1:] Rabbi Joshua ben Levi said, "The scriptural foundation for the position of rabbis is that after all the commandments, it then is written, 'You speak with us, and we will hear'" (Ex. 20:16).
>
> B. How does Rabbi Joshua ben Levi explain this verse?
>
> C. He rejects the view that temporal order does not pertain to the Torah,
>
> D. Or perhaps the statement, "You speak with us and we will hear" applies only after every two or three of the Ten Commandments.

3.D speaks of the number of commandments, and No. 4 explains which commandments were said by not Moses and Aaron but God himself. And that footnote to a footnote draws us back to our base-verse.

> 4 A. Rabbi Azariah and Rabbi Judah ben Rabbi Simon in the name of Rabbi Joshua ben Levi took

his position. They said, "It is written, 'Moses commanded us the Torah' " (Dt. 33:4).

B. "In the entire Torah there are six hundred thirteen commandments. The numerical value of the letters in the word 'Torah' is only six hundred eleven. These are the ones that Moses spoke to us."

C. "But 'I [am the Lord your God]' and 'You will not have [other gods besides me]' (Ex. 20:1–2) we have heard not from the mouth of Moses but from the Mouth of the Holy One, blessed be he."

D. "That is in line with this verse: 'O that you would kiss me with the kisses of your mouth!' "

What follows will give support to those who, not understanding the rules of composition of the rabbinic literature, represent that literature as disorganized or rambling, as having no program, no order of a propositional character, no flow of argument such as we ordinarily expect in a well-composed document. But when we understand how the following set of compositions has been framed into a single composite and why the whole has been inserted here, we shall see the opposite: a sensible representation of a large and well-presented topic.

Lest readers think that I introduce a dead issue, I want to set forth a living debate as to the character of rabbinic writing—which really concerns the character of the Judaic religious system that that writing represents. It is common for scholars in the Yeshiva world, that is, the world of Orthodox Judaic learning, to represent the Talmud as disorganized, run on, agglutinative. In representing the Talmud of Babylonia, the well-known Israeli Talmud scholar, Adin Steinsaltz, writes, "The Talmud . . . deals with an overwhelmingly broad subject—the nature of all things according to the Torah. Therefore its contours are a reflection of life itself. It has no formal external order, but is bound by a strong inner connection between its many diverse subjects. . . . The authority of the Talmud lies in its use of this rigorous method in its search for truth with regard to the entire Torah—in other words, with regard to all possible subjects in the world, both physical and spiritual." So Steinsaltz alleges that the Talmud follows no "formal external order." If he were right, people should imagine

that the Talmud or the Midrash-compilations, such as the one before us, is about nothing in particular.

But in fact the two Talmuds and most of the Midrash-compilations are well-crafted and treat some few things in all their rich
particulars. And that statement pertains to the rabbinic writers'
substantive propositions, the things that, through an infinity of
details, the framers wish to show time and again. Not only is the
rabbinic literature not disorderly, it is both orderly and, in a strict
sense, wonderfully repetitious, because it says the same thing
about many things. What Steinsaltz alleges is all-encompassing is
a selective piece of writing; what he sees as essentially pointless—
the document as a whole—proves purposeful and well-crafted.
That explains why Steinsaltz is wrong, and why vast stretches of
the Bavli prove Steinsaltz is wrong.

Steinsaltz is good at explaining the meaning of words and
phrases. But when he perpetuates the notion that the Talmud or
any other rabbinic writing is formless and disorderly, about everything and its opposite, he misrepresents the document by
viewing bits and pieces without looking at the whole. In fact,
as we have seen in our Midrash-document, the Talmud, or the
Midrash-compilation, speaks in a single voice. It everywhere
speaks uniformly, consistently, and predictably. It follows rules
that govern language choice, the order of topics to be introduced,
the cogency of paragraphs set forth in sequence. These are external traits of order. The voice of any rabbinic writing is the voice
of a book. True, in the main, the document seems to intend to
provide notes, an abbreviated script which anyone may use to
reconstruct and reenact formal discussions of problems: about
this, one says that. Curt and often arcane, these notes can be translated only with lengthy explanatory inserts. All of this script of
information is public and undifferentiated, not individual and id-
iosyncratic. We must assume people took for granted that, out of
the signs of speech, it would be possible for anyone to reconstruct
speech, doing so in accurate and fully conventional ways. So the
literary traits of the document presuppose a uniform code of
communication: a single voice.

Now let us turn to the problem at hand. From Nos. 5–19 we
have a sequence of compositions that simply ignores our base-
verse. Yet the compositions individually and the composite over
all do treat the topic before us: the revelation at Sinai, the word

of God that came forth from Sinai. And since Yohanan has introduced that topic in explaining where he thinks the Song originated, the kisses came from, the topic is a legitimate one. But in our world of making books, if we have a large corpus of material that is relevant to our topic but not relevant to the proposition, what do we do with it? If we think the material sufficiently vital, we put it all together into an appendix at the end of the book. Placed into footnotes, it would divert attention from the main point. (And the reason so much academic writing is overloaded with footnotes is that the authors do lose sight of the point they wish to make.) But put at the end of the book, in an appendix, this material would enrich the book's treatment of its topic, while not impeding the powerful flow of argument and analysis. It is evidence that is relevant in general but not in particular and deserves its place outside the mainstream of discussion.

With that characterization in mind, we may make sense of Nos. 5–19. Each item is relevant in some way or other, but all of them together are irrelevant to the issue treated in our opening pages.

Do I then wish to argue that our document is perfect, that is, the best of all possible Midrash-compilations, with nothing out of place, irrelevant, or disproportionate? One can hardly make a strong case for such a proposition, when we realize that the appendix is much larger than the principal parts of the document, Nos. 1–4, themselves. I argue only that the document, viewed within the technical limits within which its writers did their work, represents the best kind of order of which they were capable.

The connection of No. 5 to No. 2 is self-evident. We have spoken of how the Word came forth from the mouth of the Holy One. How did that happen?

> 5   A. How did the Word issue forth from the mouth
>   of the Holy One, blessed be he?
>   B. Rabbi Simeon ben Yohai and rabbis:
>   C. Rabbi Simeon ben Yohai says, "It teaches that
>   the Word came forth from the right hand of
>   the Holy One, blessed be he, to the left hand
>   of the Israelites. It then made the round and
>   circumambulated the camp of Israel, a journey of
>   eighteen miles by eighteen miles, and then went

and returned from the right hand of Israel to the left hand of the Holy One, blessed be he.'"

D. "The Holy One, blessed be he, received it in his right hand and incised it on the tablets, and the sound went from one end of the world to the other: 'The voice of the Lord hews out flames of fire'" (Ps. 29:7).

E. Rabbis say, "But is there a consideration of 'left' above? And is it not written, 'Your right hand, O Lord, is glorious in power, your right hand, O Lord' (Ex. 15:6)?

F. "But the Word came forth from the mouth of the Holy One, blessed be he, from his right hand to the right hand of Israel. It then made the round and circumambulated the camp of Israel, a journey of eighteen miles by eighteen miles, and then went and returned from the right hand of Israel to the right hand of the Holy One, blessed be he."

G. "The Holy One, blessed be he, received it in his right hand and incised it on the tablets, and the sound went from one end of the world to the other: 'The voice of the Lord hews out flames of fire'" (Ps. 29:7).

6   A. Said Rabbi Berekhiah, "Rabbi Helbo repeated to me the tradition that the Word itself was inscribed on its own, and when it was inscribed, and the sound went from one end of the world to the other: 'The voice of the Lord hews out flames of fire'" (Ps. 29:7).

B. "I said to Rabbi Helbo, 'And lo, it is written, "written with the finger of God"'" (Ex. 31:18).

C. "He said to me, 'Strangler! Are you thinking of strangling me?'"

D. "I said to him, 'And what is the sense of this verse: "tables of stone, written with the finger of God"' (Ex. 31:18).

E. "He said to me, 'It is like a disciple who is written, with the master's hand guiding his hand.'"

The appendix of relevant materials moves along to a new subject, not a footnote to the foregoing, also not a reversion to the original dispute. It is simply another topical appendix. The same is to be said for the following item:

7   A. Rabbi Joshua ben Levi and rabbis:
     B. Rabbi Joshua ben Levi says, "Two Words [two of the Ten Commandments] did the Israelites hear from the mouth of the Holy One, blessed be he: 'I' and 'you will not have other gods, besides me' (Ex. 20:1–2), as it is said, 'O that you would kiss me with the kisses of your mouth,' some, but not all of the kisses [commandments]."
     C. Rabbis say, "All of the Words did the Israelites hear from the mouth of the Holy One, blessed be he."
     D. Rabbi Joshua of Sikhnin in the name of Rabbi Levi: "The scriptural basis for the position of sages is the following verse of Scripture: 'And they said to Moses, Speak with us, and we will hear'" (Ex. 20:16).
     E. How does Rabbi Joshua ben Levi interpret the verse?
     F. He differs, for considerations of temporal order do not apply in the Torah.
     G. Or perhaps the statement, "You speak with us and we will hear" applies only after every two or three of the Ten Commandments.

8   A. Rabbi Azariah and Rabbi Judah ben Rabbi Simon in the name of Rabbi Joshua ben Levi took his position. They said, "It is written, 'Moses commanded us the Torah'" (Dt. 33:4).
     B. "In the entire Torah there are six hundred thirteen commandments. The numerical value of the letters in the word 'Torah' is only six hundred eleven. These are the ones that Moses spoke to us.
     C. "But 'I [am the Lord your God]' and 'You will

not have [other gods besides me]' (Ex. 20:1–2)
we have heard not from the mouth of Moses but
from the Mouth of the Holy One, blessed be he.

D. "That is in line with this verse: 'O that you would
kiss me with the kisses of your mouth.' "

Now we return to another reading of our base-verse which is
well-situated in our topical appendix. It not only repeats what has
already been attributed to Yohanan, it also serves as an expansion
on the general themes at hand: How did God speak to Israel at
Sinai? Why did Israel insist on hearing the message from God
himself? The next set forms another topical composite on that
one theme.

9   A. Rabbi Yohanan interpreted the verse ["O that
you would kiss me with the kisses of your
mouth"] to speak of the Israelites when they
went up to Mount Sinai:

B. "The matter may be compared to the case of a
king who wanted to marry a woman, daughter of
good parents and member of a noble family. He
sent a messenger to her asking to speak with her.
She said, 'I am not worthy to be his serving girl.
But I want to hear it from his own mouth.' "

C. "When that messenger got back to the king [Si-
mon] his face was full of smiles, but what he said
was not grasped by the king."

D. "The king, who was astute, said, 'This one is full
of smiles. It would appear that she has agreed.
But what he says is not to be understood by me.
It appears that she has said, "I want to hear it
from his own mouth." ' "

E. "So the Israelites are the daughter of good parents. The messenger is Moses. The king is the
Holy One, blessed be he."

F. "At that time: 'And Moses reported the words of
the people to the Lord' " (Ex. 19:8).

G. "Then why say, 'And Moses told the words of
the people to the Lord?' " (Ex. 19:9).

H. "Since it says, 'Lo, I come to you in a thick cloud,

so that the people may hear when I speak to you, and may also believe you forever' (Ex. 19:9), therefore, 'And Moses told the words of the people to the Lord' " (Ex. 19:9).

I. "He said to him, 'This is what they have asked for.' "

J. "He said to him, 'They tell a child what he wants to hear.' "

10 A. Rabbi Phineas in the name of Rabbi Levi said, "There is a proverb that people say: 'One who has been bitten by a snake is afraid even of a rope.' "

B. "So said Moses, 'Yesterday, when I said, 'But behold, they will not believe me' (Ex. 4:1), I got what was coming to me on their account. He was struck by leprosy (Simon, p. 25, n.3). Now what am I going to do for them?' "

11 A. It was taught on Tannaite authority by Rabbi Simeon ben Yohai, "This is what they asked."

B. "They said, 'We want to see the glory of our King.' "

12 A. Rabbi Phineas in the name of Rabbi Levi: "It was perfectly obvious before the Holy One, blessed be he, that the Israelites were going to exchange his glory for another. 'They exchanged their glory for the likeness of an ox that eats grass' " (Ps. 106:20).

B. "Therefore, [Simon, p. 25: he left them no excuse for saying] so that they might not say, 'If he had shown us his glory and greatness, we should certainly have believed in him, but now that his glory and greatness has not been shown to us, we do not believe in him.' "

C. "This confirms the following: 'And enter not into judgment with your servant' " (Ps. 143:2).

13 A. Rabbi Yudan in the name of Rabbi Judah ben Rabbi Simon, Rabbi Judah, and Rabbi Nehemiah:

B. Rabbi Judah says, "When the Israelites heard, 'I am the Lord your God' (Ex. 20:1), the study of the Torah was fixed in their hearts, and they would study and not forget."

C. "They came to Moses saying, 'Our lord, Moses, you serve as intermediary, the messenger between us [and God]: 'You speak with us, and we will hear' (Ex. 20:16), 'now therefore why should we die' (Dt. 5:22). Who gains if we perish?'"

D. "Then they would study and forget what they have learned."

E. "They said, 'Just as Moses is mortal and passes on, so his learning passes away.'"

F. "Then they came again to Moses, saying to him, 'Our lord, Moses, would that he would reveal it to us a second time.' 'O that you would kiss me with the kisses of your mouth!' 'Would that the learning of Torah would be set in our hearts as it was before.'"

G. "He said to them, 'That cannot be now, but it will be in the age to come.'"

H. "For it is said, 'I will put my Torah in their inner part, and on their heart I shall write it'" (Jer. 31:33).

I. Rabbi Nehemiah said, "When the Israelites heard the word, 'You will not have other gods besides me,' the impulse to do evil was uprooted from their hearts."

J. "They came to Moses and said to him, 'Our lord, Moses, you serve as intermediary, the messenger between us [and God]: 'You speak with us, and we will hear' (Ex. 20:16), '. . . now therefore why should we die' (Dt. 5:22). Who gains if we perish?'"

K. "Forthwith the impulse to do evil came back."

L. "Then they came again to Moses, saying to him, 'Our lord, Moses, would that he would reveal it to us a second time.' 'O that you would kiss me with the kisses of your mouth!'"

M. "He said to them 'That cannot be now, but it will be in the age to come.'"

N. "For it is said, 'And I will take away the stony heart out of your flesh' " (Ez. 36:26).

14   A. Rabbi Azariah, and some say Rabbi Eliezer and Rabbi Yosé ben Rabbi Hanina and rabbis:

B. Rabbi Eliezer says, "The matter may be compared to the case of a king who had a wine cellar."

C. "The first guest came to him first, and he mixed a cup for him and gave it to him."

D. "A second came and he mixed a cup for him and gave it to him."

E. "When the son of the king came, he gave him the whole cellar."

F. "So the First Man was commanded in respect to seven commandments."

G. "That is in line with this verse: 'And the Lord God commanded the man, saying, You may freely eat of every tree of the garden, but the tree of the knowledge of good and evil you shall not eat, for in the day that you eat of it you shall die' " (Gen. 2:16).

The mention of Gen. 2:16 for the framers triggers an interest in that matter, and what follows is a footnote to the composition that precedes, that is, we have an appendix with its own footnote.

15   A. ["And the Lord God commanded the man, saying, 'You may freely eat of every tree of the garden, [but of the tree of the knowledge of good and evil you shall not eat, for in the day that you eat of it you shall die]' " (Gen. 2:16).]

B. [Gen. Rabbi XVI:vi.1B adds:] Rabbi Levi said, "He made him responsible to keep six commandments."

C. "He commanded him against idolatry, in line with this verse: 'Because he willingly walked after idols' " (Hos. 5:11).

D. " 'The Lord' indicates a commandment against blasphemy, in line with this verse: 'And he who blasphemes the name of the Lord' " (Lev. 24:16).

E. " 'God' indicates a commandment concerning setting up courts [and a judiciary]: 'You shall not revile the judges' " [in the verse at hand, 'God'] (Ex. 22:27).

F. " '. . . the man' refers to the prohibition of murder: 'Whoever sheds man's blood' " (Gen. 9:6).

G. " '. . . saying' refers to the prohibition of fornication: 'Saying, "If a man put away his wife" ' (Jer. 3:1).

H. " 'Of every tree you may eat' (Gen. 2:16) indicates that he commanded him concerning theft. [There are things one may take, and there are things one may not take.]"

16   A. [Continuing Eliezer's statement, 14:G:] "As to Noah, a further commandment was assigned to him, not eating a limb cut from a living animal: 'Only flesh with the life thereof which is the blood thereof' " (Gen. 9:4).

B. "As to Abraham, a further commandment was assigned to him, circumcision."

C. "Isaac devoted the eighth day to that rite."

D. "As to Jacob, a further commandment was assigned to him, the prohibition of the sinew of the thigh vein: 'Therefore the children of Israel do not eat the sinew of the thigh vein' " (Gen. 32:33).

E. "As to Judah, a further commandment was assigned to him, levirate marriage: 'And Judah said to Onan, Go into your brother's wife and perform the duty of a husband's brother for her' " (Gen. 38:8).

F. "The Israelites, by contrast, made their own all of the religious duties, positive and negative alike."

17   A. Rabbi Yosé ben Rabbi Hanina and rabbis say, "The matter may be compared to the case of a king who was divvying up rations to his legions through his generals, officers, and commanders."

B. "But when the turn of his son came, he gave him his rations with his own hand."

18 A. Rabbi Isaac says, "The matter may be compared to a king who was eating sweetmeats,"

B. "And when the turn of his son came, he gave him his rations with his own hand."

19 A. Rabbis says, "The matter may be compared to the case of a king who was eating meat."

B. "And when the turn of his son came, he gave him his rations with his own hand."

C. And some say, "He took it out of his mouth and gave it to him: 'For the Lord gives wisdom, out of his mouth comes knowledge and discernment'" (Prov. 2:6).

The appendix has come to a conclusion in its own footnote. In a well-ordered writing set forth within the technical limitations that govern here, we should expect completely fresh material, and that is precisely what we find. And yet, the reversion to our base-verse marks only one aspect of the matter. What is actually said is so remote from the sense imputed to the base-verse at Nos. 1–4 that the material now before us is simply another free-standing appendix; it is relevant to the topic, but remote from the proposition with which we commenced.

20 A. Rabbi Abbahu, and some say the following in the name of Rabbi Judah, and Rabbi Nehemiah:

B. Rabbi Nehemiah said, "[The matter of 'O that you would kiss me with the kisses of your mouth!' may be compared to] two colleagues who were occupied with teachings of the law. This one states a general principle of law, and that one states a general principle of law."

C. "Said the Holy One, blessed be he, 'Their source is through my power.'" [Simon, p. 28: "Their source comes from me."]

D. Rabbi Judah said, "Even as to the breath that comes forth from one's mouth, as you say, 'But Job does open his mouth with a breath' (Job 35:16), said the Holy One, blessed be he, 'Their source is through my power.'" [Simon, p. 28: "Their source comes from me."]

E. Rabbis say, "The souls of these are going to be taken with a kiss."

The final entry is comparable to the foregoing: yet another appendix. These items cannot have been placed after No. 4, for obvious reasons, so the framer of the whole had no choice but to tack them on at the very end.

21   A. Said Rabbi Azariah, "We find that the soul of Aaron was taken away only with a kiss: 'And Aaron the priest went up to Mount Hor at the mouth of the Lord and died there'" (Num. 33:38).

B. "How do we know the same in the case of the soul of Moses? 'So Moses the servant of the Lord died there ... according to the mouth of the Lord'" (Dt. 34:5).

C. "How do we know the same in the case of the soul of Miriam? 'And Miriam died there' (Num. 30:1). And just as 'there' in the former passages means, 'by the mouth of the Lord,' so here too the fact is the same."

D. "But it would have been inappropriate to say it explicitly."

E. "How do we know the same in the case of the soul of all the righteous? 'O that you would kiss me with the kisses of your mouth!'"

F. "[The sense is,] 'If you have occupied yourself with teachings of the Torah, so that your lips are [Simon, p. 28: "Their source comes from me."] well armed with them, then, at the end, everyone will kiss you on your mouth.'"

Let us now reconsider the entire composite of II:ii.1–21. The whole point of including II:ii.1.B through 4 is at 4.D. Without that reversion to the base-verse, we must be mystified by the inclusion of the entire composition at this particular point, since it has no bearing upon the base-verse at all. The disagreement between Yohanan and the sages' concerns whether an angel carried the Ten Commandments or whether the Word—the Ten Commandments—went on its own. If we had to choose a base-verse for the present composition, absent our base-verse of course, it would obviously have to be Dt. 4:25/Dt. 4:9. The interpolation of No. 2 may be ignored, and No. 3 expands on No. 1. No. 4, then, is continuous with No. 3 and serves very well. So the whole has been composed in connection with the requirements of Dt. 4:9, 25, and then the revisions for insertion here are minimal. But that has not prevented the framers from adding on the immense secondary exposition of the manner in which the Ten Commandments came out of God's mouth, No. 5ff. The reason is not farfetched, however, since the base-verse and the theme of the passage at hand surely justify raising such a secondary question of amplification. That is, if we read God's kisses as a reference to the Ten Commandments, then we are going to ask how the "kisses" came out of God's mouth. That accounts for the continuation at No. 7, with No. 8 tacked on as before.

Nos. 9–13 then, carry forward the theme of the revelation at Sinai, introduced as it is by the verse at hand. No. 13 happens to appeal to our base-verse, but that is in the context of an ongoing exposition, and the composition, which is first-class, cannot be credited to the ultimate redactors of our document merely because our base-verse makes its appearance. The story can have worked very well without Song 1:2, and it is at least plausible that the base-verse was inserted later; it certainly does not flow within F, where it first occurs. Nos. 14–15 are here to illustrate the greater intimacy implied in the words "his mouth" (see Simon, p. 27, n. 4). While No. 15 continues the exposition of Gen. 2:16 that is integral to No. 14, it is in fact a free-standing composition, which is why I present it separately. But that requires duplicating Gen. 2:16 for clarity. Then No. 14 continues at Nos. 16–19. I treat as distinct entries those assigned to the others listed at 14.A. The point of No. 20 has no bearing on the foregoing, but it does address our base-verse, now with a quite different focus. The point emerges only where No. 21 expands the point of 20.E.

Seeing the composite, II:i.1–21 as a whole, we may revert to the question, did this document accumulate over the years, or has it been arranged in accord with a plan formulated later to take control of a vast amount of accumulated materials and impose a single plan on the whole? It seems to me that the placing of the appendix, the insertion, at just the right point, of footnote materials, for both the appendix and the body of the text itself, the inclusion of miscellaneous items at the end, Nos. 20–21, all points to a single plan of organization. It is clear that, over time, a variety of sayings—Rabbi X says about verse Y—accumulated. We don't know who wrote them or whether they were handed on by oral or written means. We only know that, until they served the purpose of an authorship planning a coherent piece of writing, they circulated aimlessly as episodes of wisdom, bits and pieces of inert information. It is equally clear that when someone decided to formulate a systematic "commentary" to Song of Songs, that writer drew together whatever was around.

But only when that writer (or set of writers) determined what he wished to accomplish did the episodic pieces of information emerge as candidates for inclusion. The person who made the whole also dictated the inclusion of the parts. Creating a collage, he formed a statement of his own. Whatever the intent of the original authority behind a saying or even a composition made up of several sayings, it is the framer of the whole who has given us the message—and the only message—of Song of Songs Rabbah. Before that point, there was an attitude and a premise about the scriptural poetry. After that point, there was a complete, documented, insistent statement, in so many words, of the proposition that the poetry was to convey.

Up to now we have concentrated on the tableau of images that our verse conjures. Now we turn to the words of which the verse is made up. The word for kiss is made up of the letters *SH, Q,* and *N.* Now the letters that make up that word yield other meanings altogether, and the next composite, II:iv.1ff works on those meanings, drawing them back to our original passage. That is to say, we proceed to plays on words that the words of our base-verse yield. These are, "arm me," "purify me," "make me cleave to him." All of these senses now are imputed, so that another nuance is given to the love relationship. II:iii.1A–B makes the general proposition public, and II:iii.C then states the first of the three theses. Then No. 2 clarifies the foregoing, making explicit the sense of "arm," meaning, "arm with weapons of the Torah."

II:iii.1   A. Another explanation of the verse, "O that you would kiss me with the kisses of your mouth! [For your love is better than wine]":

B. "Let him arm me, purify me, make me cleave to him."

C. "Let him arm me:" "They were armed with bows and could use both the right hand and the left" (1 Chr. 12:2).

2　A. Said Rabbi Simeon ben Rabbi Nahman, "The words of Torah are to be compared to weapons."

B. "Just as weapons protect their owners in wartime, so words of Torah protect those who work sufficiently hard at learning them."

C. Rabbi Hana ben Rabbi Aha brings proof from the following verse for the same proposition: " 'Let the high praises of God be in their mouth and a double-edged sword in their hand' " (Ps. 149:6):

D. "Just as a sword consumes on both its edges, so the Torah gives life in this world and life in the world to come."

Once we have joined "kiss me" to "arm me" to "arm me with words of the Torah," we proceed to revert to our original verse: "kiss me with the kisses of his mouth." How does the Torah involve "kisses with the mouth"?

3　A. Rabbi Judah, Rabbi Nehemiah, and rabbis:

B. Rabbi Judah says, "The Torah, which was said with one mouth, was said with many mouths."

C. Rabbi Nehemiah said, "Two Torahs were stated, one by mouth [that is, memorized through oral repetition], one in writing."

D. Rabbis say, "It is because they make a decree on creatures above and they do it, on creatures below and they do it." [Simon, p. 29: "[The Torah is said to have many mouths] because its students impose their will on the beings of the upper world and on the beings of the lower world."]

E. Rabbi Joshua of Sikhnin in the name of Rabbi Levi said, "The scriptural verse that supports the position of rabbis is as follows: 'For they were princes of holiness and princes of God' " (1 Chr. 24:5).

F. " 'Princes of holiness:' these are the ministering

angels, thus: 'Therefore I have profaned the
princes of the sanctuary' " (Is. 43:28).

G. " 'And princes of God:' this refers to Israel, thus,
    'I said, "You are godlike beings" ' (Ps. 82:6).

H. " 'They make a decree on creatures above and
    they do it, on creatures below and they do it:' for
    they carry out their deeds in a state of cultic
    cleanness."

The basic point here concerns the meanings to be imputed to
the letters that spell out "kiss," and, as we know from the foregoing, among the available meanings is "arm." That accounts for
the sense important at No. 1, which then accounts for the addition of No. 2. No. 3 then works on the notion of the Torah
having many mouths, provoked by the introduction of the Torah
as a double-edged sword. To allude briefly to the question of the
history of our text, a process of agglutination would not allow the
formation of so singular and correct an order of presentation:
this, then that, then the other thing, in the sole intelligible sequence. There is no interest, in the sequence from Nos. 1–3, in
the temporal order of authorities. So, as before, if a process of agglutination over time does govern, then to begin with an outline
with blank spaces has to have been prepared and set forth for centuries to come, until someone came along to fill in a blank.

II:iv.1   A. Another explanation of the verse, "O that you
              would kiss me with the kisses of your mouth!
              [For your love is better than wine]":

          B. "Let him purify me, make me cleave to him, let
              him kiss me."

          C. "Let him purify me:" like a man who joins to-
              gether ["kisses"] the water in two cisterns to one
              another and makes them cleave together [and so
              forms of them a valid immersion-pool].

          D. That is in line with the usage in the following
              verse: "Like the joining of cisterns he joins it"
              (Is. 33:4).

We now work on the sense of the consonants used for "kiss"
that yield "run," "join." That accounts for No. 1, who runs water

from cistern to cistern and so forms of the two a valid immersion pool for purifying unclean objects. That is to say, when we have two immersion pools and we want to form one single pool, we connect the water of one with that of the other, through a channel for instance, and we say that the water of the one kisses the water of the other. The usage in Is. 33:4 has dictated that sense.

Now to the third of the three meanings imputed to the word in the base-verse:

II:v.1   A. Another explanation of the verse, "O that you would kiss me with the kisses of your mouth!":

B. "Let him kiss me, let him make me cleave to him."

C. That is in line with the usage in this verse: "The noise of the wings of the living creatures as they touched one another" (Ez. 3:13).

2   A. Another explanation of the verse, "O that you would kiss me [with the kisses of your mouth]":

B. Let him make for me the sound of kissing with his mouth.

The interest now is in the sense of the consonants used for "cleave," shown in 1.C for B. No. 2 works on the simple sense of "kiss" that the same consonants produce.

We have completed our exposition of the key word, "kiss." Another problem is the correct wording of the passage, and that involves knowing whether the "your" of "your love" is masculine or feminine. What follows is a passage of the Mishnah (Mishnah-tractate Abodah Zarah 2:5A–K) at which that question is addressed. I give the passage as it occurs in the Mishnah in bold face type, with some lines that appear only in Song of Songs Rabbah in regular type. What is in Aramaic is in italics.

II:vi.1   A. "For your love is better than wine": *There we have learned in the Mishnah [following the version in the Mishnah, which differs slightly from the version before us:]* **Said Rabbi Judah, "Rabbi Ishmael asked Rabbi Joshua as they were going along the road."**

B. "He said to him, 'On what account did they prohibit cheese made by gentiles?' "

C. "He said to him, 'Because they curdle it with rennet from carrion.' "

D. "He said to him, 'And is not the rennet from a whole offering subject to a more stringent rule than rennet from carrion, and yet they have said, "A priest who is not squeamish sucks it out raw?" ' [That is not deemed as an act of sacrilege, even though the priests have no right to any part of a whole offering; hence the rennet is deemed null. Why then take account of rennet in the present circumstance, which is, after all, of considerably less weight than the sin of sacrilege?]"

E. For Rabbi Simeon ben Laqish said, "They treated it as one who drinks from a dirty cup. While, on the one side, one may derive no benefit from such a cup that belongs to the cult, yet one also is not liable for having violated the rule against sacrilege in making use of that cup."

F. [Lacking in Song:] (But they did not concur with him and ruled, "It is not available for [the priests'] benefit, while it also is not subject to the laws of sacrilege.")

G. [Lacking in Song:] [Judah resumes his narrative:] "He went and said to him, 'Because they curdle it with rennet of calves sacrificed to idols.' "

H. [Lacking in Song:] "He said to him, 'If so, then why have they not also extended the prohibition affecting it to the matter of deriving benefit from it?' "

I. "He moved him on to another subject."

J. "He said to him, 'Ishmael, my brother, How do you read the verse: "For your [masculine] love is better than wine," or, "Your [feminine] love is better than wine" ' (Song 1:2)?

K. "He said to him, ' "For your [feminine] love is better than wine." ' "

> L. **"He said to him, 'The matter is not so. For its neighbor teaches concerning it, "Your [masculine] ointments have a goodly fragrance"'** (Song 1:3) [M. Abodah Zarah 2:5A–K].
> M. But why did he not tell him the reason [H, instead of just changing the subject, I]?
> N. Said Rabbi Jonathan, "It is because it was only recently that they had made the ruling, and Rabbi Ishmael was junior."

M–N form a little *talmud* to the foregoing, that is, a critical analysis of a proposition, presented as a moving argument, going from point to point (this is often called "dialectical") on a single line of inquiry. So we proceed to ask a question that a discerning reader will raise. Since we are then told that the reason we are not given the reason is that the speaker was just a novice who was not ready to learn it, we now are supplied with an appendix on the general theme of not telling the young things they are not ready to know.

> 2 A. Rabbi Simeon ben Halafta and Rabbi Haggai in the name of Rabbi Samuel ben Rabbi Nahman: "It is written, 'The lambs will be for your clothing'" (Prov. 27:26).
>   B. "What is actually written may be read 'hidden,' yielding the meaning, 'when your disciples are junior, you should hear from them words of Torah. When they grow up and become disciples of sages, you may reveal to them the secrets of the Torah.'"
> 3 A. Rabbi Simeon ben Yohai taught on Tannaite authority: "'Now these are the ordinances which you shall set before them'" (Ex. 21:1).
>   B. "[Since the consonants in 'set' may yield 'treasure,' we interpret in this way:] just as a treasure is not shown to any one who comes along, so is the case with teachings of the Torah."

Our talmud, made up of the compositions of Nos. 4–6, now resumes with the same question, with other answers given, pursuing essentially the same line of thought.

4 A. Rabbi Huna raised the question, and Rabbi Hama ben Uqba presented the same as an objection [to 1.M's response to 1.H:] "If his intention was only to put him off, he should have put him off with one of the five equivalent points of unclarity in the Torah, which are [Simon, p. 31:] 'uplifting, cursed, tomorrow, almond-shaped, and arise.' "

 B. "['uplifting':] do we read 'If you do well, will it not be lifted up?' (Gen. 4:7), or 'It is incurring sin if you do not do well?' " (Gen. 4:7)" [That is another example of a point of unclarity in Scripture. He did not have to choose the one he chose. The others are not specified here.]"

 C. Said Rabbi Tanhuma, "I have another [a sixth]: 'The sons of Jacob came in from the field when they heard it' (Gen. 34:7), or, 'When they heard it, the men were grieved' " (Gen. 34:7–8) [where is the break between the two sentences?].

5 A. Said Rabbi Isaac, "It is written, 'And me did the Lord command' " (Dt. 4:14).

 B. " 'There are matters that he said to me, all by myself, and there are matters that he said to me to say to his children.' "

6 A. [Following Simon, p. 31, n. 2, the point of reference in what follows is our base-verse, "O that you would kiss me with the kisses of your mouth! For your love is better than wine]": Said Rabbi Ila, "There are matters about which one's [Simon:] lips are sealed." [Simon, p. 31, n. 2: It was for this reason that he put him off with the verse, because "let him kiss me" may also mean, "let him seal my lips," and thus he hinted by this quotation that not everything is to be explained.]

 B. "How so? One verse of Scripture says, 'Your word have I laid up in my heart, that I might not sin against you' (Ps. 119:11), while another verse says, 'With my lips have I told all the ordinances of your mouth' (Ps. 119:13). How hold the two together?

C. "So long as Ira the Jairite was the master of David, he observed the verse, 'Your word have I laid up in my heart, that I might not sin against you' (Ps. 119:11), but after he died, then he followed this verse: 'With my lips have I told all the ordinances of your mouth' " (Ps. 119:13).

Here is a classic case of parachuting a complete composition that in no way serves the interest of a sustained reading of a base document. The only reason that this entire talmud has been inserted here is that our base-verse forms part of the whole. But nothing that is said about our base-verse fits together with any of the prevailing points of interest, let alone important propositions. It is perfectly routine for framers of documents of the present type to collect everything they can in which the base-verses appear, even though what they gather has been made up for purposes quite different from the ones that define the document under aggregation.

We now move on to a separate theme, comparing "love" to words of Torah, with the sense of "love" as "loved ones," hence, "words of Torah." So the topical exposition moves from the senses imputed to the word "kiss" to the meaning of "love," with the clear understanding that the expression of God's love is the provision of words of the Torah. That forms the premise behind II:vii.1.

II:vii.1 A. "For your love is better than wine":

B. Words of Torah complement one another, friends of one another, close to one another,

C. In line with the usage [of the consonants that are translated "love"] in the following verse: "or his uncle or his uncle's son" (Lev. 25:49).

2 A. [Supply: water removes uncleanness, when the water is of the correct classification:] "But a fountain or cistern wherein is a gathering of water" (Lev. 11:36).

B. Water imparts susceptibility to uncleanness: "If water be put on seed" (Lev. 11:38). [The point of the juxtaposition is that while water can remove uncleanness, water can also impart

susceptibility to uncleanness. The relationship of
the two verses shows how words of Torah "complement one another, friends of one another,
close to one another."]

The appendix is topical, not propositional; we have no need to
expound the proposition about "love" and "words of Torah" to
ask about the place of "words of scribes" in God's scheme of
things, as follows:

3   A. Simeon ben Rabbi Abba in the name of Rabbi
        Yohanan: "Words of scribes are as precious as
        words of the Torah."
     B. "What is the scriptural basis for that view? [Fol-
        lowing Simon:] 'And the roof of your mouth like
        the best wine [Simon, p. 32, n. 3: The roof of the
        mouth is taken as a symbol of the Oral Torah and
        wine as a symbol of the written Torah.]'"
     C. Colleagues in the name of Rabbi Yohanan:
        "Words of scribes are more precious than words
        of Torah: 'For your love is better than wine'"
        (Song 1:2).
     D. "If one says, 'there is no requirement as to phy-
        lacteries,' so as to violate the requirements of the
        explicit words of the Torah, he is exempt from li-
        ability."
     E. "If he says, 'There is a requirement that the phy-
        lacteries contain five [not four] compartments,'
        intending thereby to add to the requirements of
        the teachings of the scribes, by contrast, he is lia-
        ble to a penalty."
4   A. Rabbi Abba ben Rabbi Kahana in the name of
        Rabbi Judah ben Pazzi derived the same lesson
        from the following:
     B. Said Rabbi Tarfon, "I was coming along the
        road [in the evening] and reclined to recite the
        Shema as required by the House of Shammai.
        And [in doing so] I placed myself in danger of
        [being attacked by] bandits." [They said to him,
        "You are yourself responsible [for what might

have befallen you], for you violated the words of the House of Hillel.'"] [M. Berakhot 1:3G–H].

C. You see that had he not recited the Shema at all, he would have violated a positive commandment alone. Now that he has recited the Shema, he has become liable for his life.

D. That proves that Words of scribes are more precious than words of Torah.

5 A. Rabbi Hanina ben Rabbi Aha in the name of Rabbi Tanhum ben Rabbi Aha said, "They are subject to more stringent penalties than the words of the Torah and of the prophets."

B. "It is written, 'Do not preach, they preach'" (Mic. 2:6). [Simon, p. 32, n. 9: implying that prophecy can be interrupted, but not so the teaching of the sages.]

C. "[The relationship of teachings of scribes and prophets] yields the following simile: the matter may be compared to the case of a king who sent his agents to a town. Concerning one of them he wrote, 'If he shows you my seal and signature, believe him, and if not, do not believe him,' and concerning the other of them he wrote, 'Even if he does not show you my seal and signature, believe him.'"

D. "So in connection with teachings of prophecy: 'If there arise in your midst a prophet . . . and he gives you a sign'" (Dt. 13:2).

E. "But as to words of scribes: 'According to the Torah that they will teach you'" (Dt. 17:11).

F. "What is written is not, 'according to the Torah that the Torah will teach you,' but 'according to the Torah that they will teach you.'"

G. "What is written is not, 'according to the judgment that it will tell you,' but '. . . that they shall tell you.'"

H. "Further: 'You shall not turn aside from the sentence that they shall declare to you to either the right hand or to the left'" (Dt. 17:11).

I. "If they tell you that the right hand is right and

the left hand is left, obey; and even if they tell
you that the right hand is left and the left hand is
right!"

Once more let us see things whole. The point of Nos. 1 and 2
is clear; No. 2 illustrates No. 1. The word for "love" is now under
examination. A play on the word for "love" yields "roof of your
mouth," and the entirety of what follows is added for that reason.
The point now is to compare the oral Torah with the written, and
that yields the comparison of teachings of scribes ("sages" in Simon's translation) and teachings of the written Torah. We start
with the claim that the two are equal, No. 3, and move on for the
rest to the allegation that teachings of scribes or of the oral Torah
are more to be valued and are subject to more severe penalties.

The general theme of words of Torah as expressions of God's
love, invited by "your love is better than wine," is made particular. In this context we have compared words of Torah to wine, so
we consider the analogies for words of Torah: wine, oil, honey,
milk, all of them spelled out. Here, our base-verse and its exposition contributes to the formation of a composition that has its
own point of interest, namely, analogies for words of Torah. The
base-verse itself is not expounded, as follows:

II:viii.1   A. Another explanation of the verse, "For your love
                is better than wine":
            B. Words of the Torah are compared to water,
                wine, oil, honey, and milk.
       2   A. To water: "Ho, everyone who thirsts come for
                water" (Is. 55:1).
            B. Just as water is from one end of the world to the
                other, "To him who spread forth the earth above
                the waters" (Ps. 136:6), so the Torah is from one
                end of the world to the other, "The measure
                thereof is longer than the earth" (Job 11:9).
            C. Just as water is life for the world, "A fountain of
                gardens, a well of living waters" (Song 4:15), so
                the Torah is life for the world, "For they are life
                to those who find them and health for all their
                flesh" (Prov. 4:22); "Come, buy and eat" (Is.
                55:1).
            D. Just as water is from heaven, "At the sound of his

giving a multitude of waters in the heavens" (Jer. 10:13), so the Torah is from heaven, "I have talked with you from heaven" (Ex. 20:19).

E. Just as water [when it rains] is with loud thunder, "The voice of the Lord is upon the water" (Ps. 29:3), so the Torah is with loud thunder, "And it came to pass on the third day, when it was morning, that there were thunderings and lightnings" (Ex. 19:16).

F. Just as water restores the soul, "But God cleaves the hollow place which was in Levi and water came out, and when he had drunk, he revived" (Judges 15:19), so the Torah restores the soul, "The Torah of the Lord is perfect, restoring the soul" (Ps. 19:8).

G. Just as water purifies a person from uncleanness, "And I will sprinkle clean water upon you, and you will be clean" (Ez. 36:25), so the Torah cleans a person of uncleanness, "The words of the Lord are pure" (Ps. 12:7).

H. Just as water cleans the body, "He shall bathe himself in water" (Lev. 17:15), so the Torah cleans the body, "Your word is purifying to the uttermost" (Ps. 119:140).

I. Just as water covers over the nakedness of the sea, "As the waters cover the sea" (Is. 11:9), so the Torah covers the nakedness of Israel, "Love covers all transgressions" (Prov. 10:12).

J. Just as water comes down in drops but turns into rivers, so too the Torah—a person learns two laws today, two tomorrow, until he becomes an overflowing river.

K. Just as water, if one is not thirsty, has no sweetness in it, so the Torah, if one does not labor at it, has no sweetness in it.

L. Just as water leaves the height and flows to a low place, so the Torah leaves one who is arrogant on account of [his knowledge of] it and cleaves to one who is humble on account of [his knowledge of] it.

M. Just as water does not keep well in utensils of

silver and gold but only in the most humble of utensils, so the Torah does not stay well except in the one who treats himself as a clay pot.

N. Just as with water, a great man is not ashamed to say to an unimportant person, "Give me a drink of water," so as to words of Torah, the great man is not ashamed to say to an unimportant person, "Teach me a chapter," or "a verse," or even "a single letter."

O. Just as with water, when one does not know how to swim in it, in the end he will be swallowed up, so words of Torah, if one does not know how to swim in them and to give instruction in accord with them, in the end he will be swallowed up.

P. Said Rabbi Hanina of Caesarea, "Just as water is drawn not only for gardens and orchards, but also for baths and privies, shall I say that that is so also for words of the Torah?"

Q. "Scripture says, 'For the ways of the Lord are right'" (Hos. 14:10).

R. Said Rabbi Hama ben Uqba, "Just as water makes plants grow, so words of the Torah make everyone who works in them sufficiently grow."

S. Then [may one say,] just as water becomes rancid and smelly in a vessel, so words of the Torah are the same way? Scripture says that the Torah is like wine. Just as with wine, so long as it ages in the bottle, it improves, so words of the Torah, so long as they age in the body of a person, they improve in stature.

T. Then [may one say,] just as water is not to be discerned in the body, so is the case with words of the Torah? Scripture says that the Torah is like wine. Just as with wine, its presence is discerned when it is in the body, so words of the Torah are discerned when they are in the body.

U. [For] people hint and point with the finger, saying, "This is a disciple of a sage."

V. Then [may one say,] just as water does not make one happy, so is the case with words of the Torah? Scripture says that the Torah is like wine.

Just as wine "makes the heart of man glad" (Ps. 104:15), so words of the Torah make the heart happy, "The precepts of the Lord are right, rejoicing the heart" (Ps. 19:9).

W. Then [may one say,] just as wine sometimes is bad for the head and the body, so is the case with words of the Torah? Scripture compares words of the Torah to oil. Just as oil is pleasing for the head and body, so words of the Torah are pleasing for the head and body: "Your word is a lamp to my feet" (Ps. 119:105).

Z. May one then say, just as oil is bitter to begin with, and sweet only at the end, so is it the case also with words of Torah? Scripture states, "Honey and milk" (Song 4:11). Just as they are sweet, so words of the Torah are sweet: "Sweeter than honey" (Ps. 19:11).

AA. May one then say, just as honey has wax cells [that cannot be eaten], so words of the Torah are the same? Scripture says, "milk" (Song 4:11). Just as milk is pure, so words of the Torah are pure: "Gold and glass cannot equal it" (Job 28:17).

BB. May one then say, just as milk is [Simon:] insipid, so words of the Torah are the same? Scripture states, "Honey and milk" (Song 4:11). Just as honey and milk, when they are stirred together, do not do any harm to the body, so words of the Torah: "It shall be health to your navel" (Prov. 3:8); "For they are life to those who find them" (Prov. 4:22).

The composition is sustained and perfect. The comparison of "your love," understood as "words of the Torah," to wine persuaded the compositors that the entire piece belongs. But of course it has not been written out to serve our base-verse in particular, nor any other. It is a free-standing and powerful composition, making its own point about its own subject, and not an amplification in terms of another set of values of a given verse and its contents.

A new set of verbal symbols is now introduced at II:ix.1ff.

These analogies really draw us back to our starting point at Nos. II:i.1–4. We interrupted our exposition of the verse and its analogies, and now we resume with an astonishing, nearly mute sequence of "another matter"-statements.

II:ix.1 A. Another explanation of the verse, "For your love is better: . . ."
 B. This refers to the patriarchs.
 C. "than wine":
 D. This refers to the princes.

2 A. Another explanation of the verse, "For your love is better: . . ."
 B. This refers to the offerings.
 C. "than wine":
 D. This refers to the libations.

3 A. Said Rabbi Hanina, "If when the Israelites came to that awful deed, Moses had known how precious were the offerings, he would have offered all of the offerings that are catalogued in the Torah.
 B. "Instead he ran to the merit of the patriarchs: 'Remember Abraham, Isaac, and Israel, your servants'" (Ex. 32:13).

4 A. Another explanation of the verse, "For your love is better: . . ."
 B. This refers to Israel.
 C. "than wine":
 D. This refers to the gentiles.
 E. "[For the numerical value of the letters that make up the word for wine] is seventy,"
 F. "teaching you that the Israelites are more precious before the Holy One, blessed be he, than all of the nations."

The composition, with its footnote at No. 3, is a powerful triplet, in which the more valuable is compared with the less valuable: first patriarchs and princes, then offerings and merit, finally Israel and the nations. That the whole is inseparable and unitary is shown by the climax, No. 4, and that becomes obvious because of the interpolation at No. 3. So the whole, inclusive of

No. 3, is aiming at the final point, 4.F. That is just where we began our exposition of "your love is better . . ."—the love of Israel is better. Through a mass of detail, a single thread of argument holds the whole together. And that thread, clear only at the outer fringe of the tapestry, has formed the focus of our vision all along: the premise becomes the conclusion.

3

Song of Songs Rabbah to Song of Songs 1:5

I am very dark, but comely,
O daughters of Jerusalem,
like the tents of Kedar,
like the curtains of Solomon.

The protracted and complex literary composite considered in the previous chapter is less characteristic of Song of Songs Rabbah than the one discussed in this chapter. Here we have a long sequence of symbols in words, joined to the elements of a verse of Scripture. The verse before us sets up a contrast, "dark, but comely." Israel now speaks. "Dark" represents Israel's bad side, "comely," the good side. We then have a chance to contrast Israel's failures with its surpassing moments of love for God and loyalty to God. The message is both general and particular. Israel rebels, sinning or showing little faith, but it also obeys, acting in accord with God's will. Here we see how "another matter" serves as a means of laying out a sequence of portraits, verbal symbols that are not translated into propositions but that speak without further elaboration.

V:i.1   A. "I am very dark, but comely [O daughters of Jerusalem, like the tents of Kedar, like the curtains of Solomon]" (Song 1:5):

59

       B. "I am dark" in my deeds.

       C. "But comely" in the deeds of my forebears.

2   A. "I am very dark, but comely":

       B. Said the community of Israel, " 'I am dark' in my view, 'but comely' before my Creator."

       C. For it is written, "Are you not as the children of the Ethiopians to Me, O children of Israel, says the Lord" (Amos 9:7):

       D. "as the children of the Ethiopians"—in your sight.

       E. But "to Me, O children of Israel, says the Lord."

3   A. Another interpretation of the verse, "I am very dark": in Egypt.

       B. "but comely": in Egypt.

       C. "I am very dark": in Egypt: "But they rebelled against me and would not hearken to me" (Ezr. 20:8).

       D. "but comely" in Egypt: with the blood of the Passover offering and circumcision, "And when I passed by you and saw you wallowing in your blood, I said to you, 'In your blood live' " (Ezr. 16:6)—in the blood of the Passover.

       E. "I said to you, 'In your blood live' " (Ezr. 16:6)—in the blood of the circumcision.

4   A. Another interpretation of the verse, "I am very dark": at the sea. "They were rebellious at the sea, even the Red Sea" (Ps. 106:7).

       B. "but comely": at the sea. "This is my God and I will be comely for him" (Ex. 15:2) [following Simon's rendering of the verse].

5   A. "I am very dark": at Marah. "And the people murmured against Moses, saying, What shall we drink" (Ex. 15:24).

       B. "but comely": at Marah. "And he cried to the Lord and the Lord showed him a tree, and he cast it into the waters and the waters were made sweet" (Ex. 15:25).

6   A. "I am very dark": at Rephidim. "And the name of the place was called Massah and Meribah" (Ex. 17:7).

       B. "but comely": at Rephidim. "And Moses built an

altar and called it by the name 'the Lord is my
banner' " (Ex. 17:15).

7   A. "I am very dark": at Horeb. "And they made a
         calf at Horeb" (Ps. 106:19).

     B. "but comely": at Horeb. "And they said, All that
         the Lord has spoken we will do and obey" (Ex.
         24:7).

8   A. "I am very dark": in the wilderness. "How often
         did they rebel against him in the wilderness" (Ps.
         78:40).

     B. "but comely": in the wilderness at the setting up
         of the tabernacle. "And on the day that the taber-
         nacle was set up" (Num. 9:15).

9   A. "I am very dark": in the deed of the spies. "And
         they spread an evil report of the land" (Num.
         13:32).

     B. "but comely": in the deed of Joshua and Caleb.
         "Save for Caleb, the son of Jephunneh the Keniz-
         zite" (Num. 32:12).

10   A. "I am very dark": at Shittim. "And Israel abode
         at Shittim and the people began to commit
         harlotry with the daughters of Moab" (Num.
         25:1).

     B. "but comely": at Shittim. "Then arose Phinehas
         and wrought judgment" (Ps. 106:30).

11   A. "I am very dark": through Achan. "But the chil-
         dren of Israel committed a trespass concerning
         the devoted thing" (Josh. 7:1).

     B. "but comely": through Joshua. "And Joshua said
         to Achan, My son, give I pray you glory" (Josh.
         7:19).

12   A. "I am very dark": through the kings of Israel.

     B. "but comely": through the kings of Judah.

     C. If with my dark ones that I had, it was such that
         "I am comely," all the more so with my prophets.

The contrast of dark and comely yields a variety of applica-
tions. In all of them the same situation that is the one also is the
other, and the rest follows in a wonderfully well-crafted composition. What is the point of the repertoire? Israel is dark in deeds,
comely in the deeds of the patriarchs and matriarchs; dark in

Egypt, comely in Egypt; dark at the sea, comely at the sea; dark at Marah, comely at Marah; so too Rephidim, the Wilderness, the spies vs. Joshua and Caleb; Shittim; and Achan. There is no missing the point, which is a very concrete one. Each moment in Israel's history contains within itself the possibility of rebellion or obedience, and Israel time and again has shown its mixed character. Just as in each individual the impulse to do good contends with the impulse to do evil, so Israel as a community lives out its history—the journey from Egyptian slavery to the promised land of Israel—in two planes, each one event in two dimensions. Note that history as a linear progression of single events here is transformated into something else. History is now a set of examples of rules, or laws of the social order; it is no longer a sequence of things that happen once in some set and consequential order. If we had rearranged the order of events—e.g., Achan, Shittim, the sea—the proposition would not have shifted. The events are important not because they are linear, but because they are not linear: each event is like all the others, and the whole forms a set of examples of a single prevailing proposition. So history is turned into what we should now call social science: the search for the rule that turns the unique into the exemplary.

We proceed to a different reading of the same matter, one that upsets the flow of exposition.

V:ii.1   A. "I am very dark":
          B. Scripture speaks of Ahab: "And it came to pass when Ahab heard those words that he tore his clothing and put sackcloth upon his flesh and fasted and went softly" (1 Kgs. 21:27).

2   A. How long did he afflict himself?
          B. Rabbi Joshua ben Levi said, "For three hours. If he was accustomed to eat his meal at the third hour of the day, he ate it at the sixth, and if he was accustomed to eat at the sixth, he ate at the ninth."

3   A. "And he lay in sackcloth and went softly" (1 Kgs. 21:27):
          B. Rabbi Joshua ben Levi said, "He went barefoot."

4   A. As to Jehorum, what is written?
          B. "And the people look, and behold, he had sackcloth within, upon his flesh" (1 Kgs. 6:30).

I find V:ii.1–4 disruptive, and I do not see what is accomplished by the identification of Ahab with the matter at hand. True, there is a contrast to be drawn between "dark" Ahab and "comely" Josiah (to pick one good king out of the available list), but that contrast is not drawn or even pertinent. **So we have a parachuted item.** Now we resume our exposition, and the established pattern of contrasts is reworked in other than historical terms. No proposition such as the historical, social scientific one that preceded the present one emerges.

5   A. [As to the verse, "I am very dark, but comely," Rabbi Levi ben Rabbi Haita gave four interpretations:

B. " 'I am very dark': all the days of the week."

C. " 'but comely': on the Sabbath."

D. " 'I am very dark': all the days of the year."

E. " 'but comely': on the Day of Atonement."

F. " 'I am very dark': among the Ten Tribes."

G. " 'but comely': in the tribe of Judah and Benjamin."

H. " 'I am very dark': in this world."

I. " 'but comely': in the world to come."

We have completed our exposition and proceed to the next clause in our base-verse. As in chapter 1, our movement is toward the reading of the components of the verse. We take up the word *daughters,* and the same consonants can be read as in *builders.* This allows us to speak about the builders of Jerusalem. We have left far behind the context of the Song of Songs; there is no effort now to speak of the love of God and Israel. Now the elements of sentences of the Song are read in their own terms. And yet, as we see, the setting—God's love for Israel—still defines, since we move quickly from Jerusalem back to women. Israel is compared to a woman in a concrete exposition, just as in the Song, Israel is the woman who receives God's love.

V:iii.1   A. "O daughters of Jerusalem":

B. Rabbis say, "Do not read the letters that spell out 'daughters of Jerusalem' as given, but rather, as 'builders of Jerusalem' " [since the same consonants can yield that other reading].

C. This refers to the great Sanhedrin of Israel, the court that goes into session to clarify every question and matter of judgment. ["Builders" and "clarify" have the same consonants.]

2   A. Another interpretation of the phrase, "O daughters of Jerusalem":

B. Said Rabbi Yohanan, "Jerusalem is destined to be made the metropolitan capital of all cities and [Simon:] draw people to her in streams to do her honor."

C. "That is in line with the following passage of Scripture: 'Ashdod, its towns [using the letters that spell out the word for daughters] and villages, Gaza, its town and its villages until Lesha' " (Josh. 15:47).

D. That is the view, then, of Rabbi Yohanan.

E. For Rabbi Yohanan said, "It is written, 'I will give them to you for daughters, but not because of your covenant' " (Ezr. 16:61).

F. "What is the sense of 'daughters'? It means towns."

G. "What is the sense of, 'but not because of your covenant'? 'Not on account of your contract, but as a gift from me.' "

3   A. Rabbi Bibi in the name of Rabbi Reuben said, "Sing, O barren" (Is. 54:1).

B. "Now is there a song to celebrate barrenness?"

C. "But 'sing O barren one' for you have not born children for Gehenna.' "

4   A. Rabbi Berekhiah in the name of Rabbi Samuel ben Rabbi Nahman said, "The Israelites are compared to a woman."

B. "Just as an unmarried women receives a tenth part of the property of her father and takes her leave [for her husband's house when she gets married], so the Israelites inherited the land of the seven peoples, who form a tenth part of the seventy nations of the world."

C. "And because the Israelites inherited in the status of a woman, they said a song in the feminine form of that word, as in the following: 'Then sang Moses and the children of Israel this song [given in the feminine form] unto the Lord'" (Ex. 15:1).

D. "But in the age to come they are destined to inherit like a man, who inherits all of the property of his father."

E. "That is in line with this verse of Scripture: 'From the east side to the west side: Judah, one portion . . . Dan one, Asher one . . .'" (Ezr. 48:7), and so throughout.

F. "Then they will say a song in the masculine form of that word, as in the following: 'Sing to the Lord a new song'" (Ps. 96:1).

G. "The word 'song' is given not in its feminine form but in its masculine form."

5   A. Rabbi Berekiah and Rabbi Joshua ben Levi: "Why are the Israelites compared to a woman?"

B. "Just as a woman takes up a burden and puts it down [that is, becomes pregnant and gives birth], takes up a burden and puts it down, then takes up a burden and puts it down and then takes up no further burden,"

C. "so the Israelites are subjugated and then redeemed, subjugated and then redeemed, but in the end are redeemed and will never again be subjugated."

D. "In this world, since their anguish is like the anguish of a woman in childbirth, they say the song before him using the feminine form of the word for song,"

E. "but in the age to come, because their anguish will no longer be the anguish of a woman in childbirth, they will say their song using the masculine form of the word for song":

F. "'In that day this song [in the masculine form of the word] will be sung'" (Is. 26:1).

No. 1 stands by itself in its reading of "daughters of Jerusalem." No. 2 is likewise free-standing. The remainder address the femininity of Israel in this world in contrast to its masculinity in the world to come. No. 3 sets the stage, though it seems to me not to require what follows. Nos. 4 and 5 fully exploit the possibilities of the comparison. My sense is that Solomon's address to the daughters of Jerusalem in particular is what has persuaded the compilers of the appropriateness of these materials.

We continue the exposition of the elements of the verse now with "tents of Kedar." But we read that simile in the way in which we read the contrast of "dark" and "comely." Here, the contrast is between the outside of a tent and its inside ("dark," "comely"). The simile calls to mind the Torah, now in the person of disciples of sages; then in the person of Israel as a whole.

V:iv.1   A. "like the tents of Kedar, [like the curtains of Solomon]" (Song 1:5):

B. Just as the tents of Kedar, that appear from the outside to be ugly, black, and tattered, on the inside they are made up of precious stones and pearls,

C. so disciples of sages, while they appear in this world to be ugly and black, inside they contain Torah, Scripture, Mishnah, Midrash, laws, Talmud, Tosefta, and lore.

D. Might one say just as the tents of Kedar do not need to be cleaned, the same is the case with Israel?

E. Scripture says, "like the curtains of Solomon."

F. Just as the curtains of Solomon get dirty and are cleaned and then get dirty and are cleaned again, so too the Israelites, even though they are dirty with sins all the days of the year, on the Day of Atonement, they make atonement for them:

G. "For on this day shall atonement be made for you, to cleanse you" (Lev 16:30). "Though your sins be as scarlet, they shall be white as snow" (Is. 1:18).

H. Might one say just as tents of Kedar are moved about from place to place, such is the case with Israel?

I. Scripture says, "like the curtains of Solomon."

J. They are like the tents of Him to whom peace belongs, the One at whose word the world came into being,

K. For from the moment that he stretched [his tents] forth, they never again moved from their place.

2   A. Rabbi Eliezer ben Jacob taught on Tannaite authority, "A tent that shall not be removed" (Is. 33:20):

B. "The word for 'removed' means shall not go forth and shall not stir."

3   A. Just as in the case of the tents of Kedar, the yoke of no creature is upon them,

B. So in the case of the Israelites in the age to come, the yoke of no creature will be upon them.

4   A. Rabbi Hiyya taught on Tannaite authority, " 'And I made you go upright' " (Lev. 26:13):

B. " 'Upright' means standing erect, fearful of no creature."

5   A. Rabbi Yudan said, "[Israel] is like Joseph:

B. "Just as Joseph was sold to the tents of Kedar, 'And they sold Joseph to the Ishmaelites' (Gen. 37:28), and afterward bought those who had bought him. 'So Joseph bought all the land of Egypt' " (Gen. 47:20),

C. "So the Israelites, 'will take their captors captive' " (Is. 14:2).

The exposition of the double metaphor, "tents of Kedar, curtains of Solomon," once more appeals to the metaphor to clarify the traits of Israel. The set of No. 1 breaks at D, since the initial comparison is only to disciples of sages, whereas the continuation moves directly to Israel as a whole. The rhetoric of D and beyond requires us to read No. 1 as a sustained and unitary statement, as I have presented it, however, anyone wishing to treat 1.D and what follows it as a separate entry would have good reason to do so. It seems to me that No. 2 is inserted simply because it refers to "tent," but there is no continuity between Nos. 2 and 3. Then

No. 3 carries forward the method and thought of No. 1. No. 4 is added because it has the same conception as No. 3, and No. 5 for essentially the same reason. So a single conception, the one of No. 1, stressing the freedom of the Israelites in the age to come, holds the whole together.

4

Song of Songs Rabbah to Song of Songs 2:6

O that his left hand were under my head,
and that his right hand embraced me!

The repertoire of the sacred available to our authors extended far beyond moments in an eternal present, the sea and Sinai, the Davidic monarchy and the Temple. When I said that our sages read Scripture like a personal letter from God to Israel written that morning, I had in mind a passage such as the verse at hand, which speaks of the religious life under the law of the Torah that, in the sages' mind, Israel carried on. In the reading of the present verse, we begin with the tablets of the law and proceed to the principal items of the holy life lived every day: garments bearing show-fringes *(tsitsit)* that Reform and Conservative Jews wear at prayer even now (a prayer shawl, or *tallit,* holding them) and that many Orthodox Jews wear on an undergarment all day long (on a *tallit qatan,* or small prayer shawl, worn as a kind of t-shirt). From clothing, we proceed to phylacteries *(tefillin),* boxes containing scraps of parchment on which are written verses of Scripture, worn at morning prayer on weekdays and, in the early

centuries, worn by sages all day long. The daily life of worship
proceeds to the recitation of the Shema ("Hear O Israel, the Lord
our God, the Lord is One.") and the recitation of the Prayer, that
is, the eighteen benedictions of praise, petition, and thanksgiving
recited three times a day in worship. The first reading of the verse
that refers to God's caresses of Israel, therefore, sees the acts of
donning prayer garments and reciting the morning prayer as acts
of loving communion between God and Israel. The donning of
the garments and the acts of prayer represent God's caresses of
the faithful Israelite (covering Nos. 1–3 below).

From the love of God and the pious Jew, we proceed to the
household of Judaism, that is, the everyday common home. Just
as we began with Sinai and the Ten Commandments and turned
outward to the morning worship, here too we begin with what is
considered an analogy in the sacred and move outward to the
secular world. Here the analogy is drawn from the tabernacle,
with God's presence in the wilderness, which is the model for the
Israelite home in the here and now; hence, No. 4. Then, at No.
5, we move onward to the *mezuzah,* a box containing parchments
with verses of Scripture affixed to the doorposts of the house,
entryways from the outside and rooms on the inside. Three miscellaneous entries, an appendix and two footnotes follow at Nos.
6–8. No. 6 is simply a topical appendix. Since the verse at hand
says that "the left hand" "under my head" is the mezuzah, the inclusion of No. 6, which speaks of the mezuzah at the right
doorpost, is somewhat jarring. Nos. 7 and 8, by contrast, form
quite pertinent complements, since they broaden our reading of
the base-verse. But since they violate the established form of Nos.
1–5, they are tacked on at the end—further readings of the base-
verse, and entirely appropriate ones at that.

XXIII:i.1   A. "O that his left hand were under my head":
      B. This refers to the first tablets.
      C. "and that his right hand embraced me":
      D. This refers to the second tablets.
    2   A. Another interpretation of the verse, "O that his
         left hand were under my head":
      B. This refers to the show-fringes.
      C. "and that his right hand embraced me":
      D. This refers to the phylacteries.

3 A. Another interpretation of the verse, "O that his left hand were under my head":

   B. This refers to the recitation of the Shema.

   C. "and that his right hand embraced me":

   D. This refers to the Prayer.

4 A. Another interpretation of the verse, "O that his left hand were under my head":

   B. This refers to the tabernacle.

   C. "and that his right hand embraced me":

   D. This refers to the cloud of the presence of God in the world to come: "The sun shall no longer be your light by day nor for brightness will the moon give light to you" (Is. 60:19). Then what gives light to you? "The Lord shall be your everlasting light" (Is. 60:20).

5 A. Another interpretation of the verse, "O that his left hand were under my head":

   B. This referrs to the mezuzah.

6 A. It has been taught on Tannaite authority by Rabbi Simeon ben Yohai, "And you shall write them on the doorposts of your house" (Dt. 6:9).

   B. "[Since the words for house and coming use the same consonants,] 'when you come into your house from the street' [you should have the mezuzah on the doorpost that you will see at your right, so it is affixed on the right doorpost as one enters the house.]"

7 A. Said Rabbi Yohanan, " 'And you shall set the table outside the veil and the candlestick . . . toward the south' " (Ex. 26:35). [That is, the candlestick is to be set on the left of someone entering from the east (Simon, p. 112, n. 3)].

   B. "And is that not the way? For does a person not put the candlestick down at the left, so that it will not impede his right hand?"

   C. "[And, with reference to the verse, 'O that his left hand were under my head, and that his right hand embraced me,'] does not a man put his left hand under the head and caress with the right?"

8 A. Said Rabbi Aha, "Rabbi Yohanan derives the

> evidence from this verse: 'to love the Lord your
> God . . . and to cleave to him' " (Dt. 11:22).
> B. "And what is this cleaving? It is with 'his left
> hand under my head.' "

Now to review the whole. The layout seems to me rather typical, in that the disciplined and well-composed materials come first, repeating their point through a standard sequence of topics available for metaphorization, then appending other, more miscellaneous items. Why we invoke, as our candidates for the metaphor at hand, the Ten Commandments, show-fringes and phylacteries, recitation of the Shema and the Prayer, the tabernacle and the cloud of the presence of God, and the mezuzah, seems to me clear from the very catalogue. These reach their climax in the analogy between the home and the tabernacle, the embrace of God and the presence of God. So the whole is meant to list those things that draw the Israelite near to God and make the Israelite cleave to God, as the base-verse says; hence the right hand and the left stand for the most intimate components of the life of the individual and the home with God. The remainder is added on and does not detract from the effect of the extraordinary metaphorization effected at Nos. 1–5.

By this point in our encounter with Song of Songs Rabbah, we are able to generalize on its program and traits. The paramount program clear is, as I said, a plan to simply identifying counterparts, in Israelite life, to the expressions of love between God and Israel. The Judaic faithful live a life of intimate love of God, and each of the acts of piety and prayer that the Jewish people do is an expression of that intimacy and affection. What the author of a given composition, such as is made up of Nos. 1–5, had to contribute, then, is not the premise—the Song of Songs deals with a love affair of God and Israel—or a list of original candidates for metaphorization. What that author had to do was select from an available repertoire the items that seemed appropriate and proper. We note, too, considerable care in arranging materials. First come the things basic to the reading of the verse, which are rarely propositional and commonly symbolic and evocative. Then we add secondary items, which amplify or clarify or otherwise complete the presentation. That means that the principal medium of discourse of our writers is the symbolic one, and everything else is secondary.

5

Song of Songs Rabbah to Song of Songs 3:9–10

King Solomon made himself a
palanquin, from the wood of Lebanon.
He made its posts of silver,
its back of gold, its seat of purple;
it was lovingly wrought within by
the daughters of Jerusalem.

Judaism's holy life is lived in eternal time—the sea, Sinai—and in the ongoing cycle of everyday life—the Shema, the Prayer, the show-fringes and phylacteries and doormarkers *(mezuzot)*. But the life of Israel with God takes place in the cosmos formed of heaven and earth. And all things correspond, so that what Israel does on earth represents a cosmic metaphor, and what takes place in the heavens stands for an earthly simile. This profound and far-reaching definition of the dimensions of the holy life—raising Israel off the plane of ordinary being and setting the holy people into a heightened reality—comes to expression in an extraordinary conception that the Temple of Jerusalem formed the nexus between heaven and earth. Here, where God is served through sacrifice, song, and prayer, the smoke of the altar fires bears upward the marks of Israel's faithfulness and love of God in the sweet scent of the offerings, the good odor of loyalty. Now, for the framers of our document, the place in which to make that statement is not philosophical discourse (to which, after all, animal sacrifices do not readily lend themselves, as the Christian thinkers discovered early), nor even in legal formulations of spiritual matters in terms of rules of action and restraint (though the entire divisions of the Mishnah devoted to holy things and purities address those matters). It is best said by indirection, once more through the pictorial symbols reduced to simple words as recast in our reading of Song of Songs Rabbah.

For the present context, the ideal meeting place of image and metaphor is the Temple, and therefore the name of Solomon, who built the Temple, and a reference to the Temple that he built out of the cedars of Lebanon, will provoke deep thought on the correspondence of one thing to something else. The verse at hand is read in its three clauses: (1) King Solomon made himself a palanquin from the wood of Lebanon; (2) He made its posts of silver, its back of gold, its seat of purple; (3) It was lovingly wrought within by the daughters of Jerusalem. At each point, then, we shall want to find the thing that is evoked by these metaphors. A mark of the success of our sages will be the coherence of the three items introduced at any one point, and the challenge to their ingenuity will be in linking Nos. 1–2 to No. 3. That is the point at which, in each of our readings we must move from the physical and material to the human and historical.

The task is easiest with Nos. 1–2, namely the linking of our verse to the Temple as a physical thing. This is done by citing verses of Exodus that describe components of the building and its furniture with the first two of our three clauses. Then, at No. 2, we move to the third of our clauses, where we speak of "the daughters of Jerusalem," i.e., those who study the Torah and devote their lives to it; or, more to the point, "the daughters of Jerusalem" stand for the presence of God in the Temple. As usual, these two items dance around a single point: God's presence in Israel is represented by the Torah, or by the presence itself, the same thing repeated.

XLIV:i.1 A. "He made its posts of silver":
B. This speaks of the pillars: "The hooks of the pillars and their fillets shall be of silver" (Ex. 27:10).
C. "its back of gold":
D. "And you shall overlay the boards with gold" (Ex. 26:29).

E. "its seat of purple":

F. "And you shall make a veil of blue and purple" (Ex. 26:31).

2 A. "It was lovingly wrought within by the daughters of Jerusalem":

B. Rabbi Yudan said, "This refers to the merit attained through the Torah and the merit attained through the righteous who occupy themselves with it."

C. Rabbi Azariah in the name of Rabbi Judah in the name of Rabbi Simon said, "This refers to the presence of God.

No. 3 is added on to the foregoing because it speaks of the theme just introduced, God's presence in the Temple. But the composite interrupts the flow of exposition and has to be treated as another footnote. The same is said of No. 4, which identifies the building in the wilderness of the tabernacle as the moment at which God's presence came back to earth.

3 A. One verse of Scripture says, "So that the priests could not stand to minister by reason of the cloud, for the glory of the Lord filled the house of the Lord" (1 Kgs. 8:11).

B. And another verse of Scripture says, "And the court was full of the brightness of the Lord's glory" (Ezr. 10:4).

C. How are these two verses to be harmonized?

D. Rabbi Joshua of Sikhnin in the name of Rabbi Levi: "To what is the tent of meeting comparable? To a cave open to the sea.

E. "When the sea becomes stormy, it fills the cave."

F. "The cave is filled, but the sea is undiminished."

G. "So the tent of meeting was filled with the splendor of the presence of God, while the world was undiminished of the presence of God."

4 A. When did the presence of God come to rest on the world?

B. On the day on which the tabernacle was raised

up: "And it came to pass on the day that Moses had made an end" (Num. 7:1).

We continue the exposition of the base-verse in terms of the tent of meeting, that is, reading Song 3:9–10 together as a single problem in interpretation. No. 1 works out the basic theme, and the rest is simply a secondary amplification of details. Now we proceed, at XLIII:ii.1, to the second metaphor, which is no longer the Temple or tabernacle but the ark.

XLIII:ii.1 A. [Supply: "King Solomon made himself a palanquin, from the wood of Lebanon. He made its posts of silver, its back of gold, its seat of purple; it was lovingly wrought within by the daughters of Jerusalem":]

     B. Rabbi Yudan ben Rabbi Ilai interpreted the verses as speaking of the ark:

     C. " 'a palanquin': this is the ark."

  2 A. [Supply: "a palanquin":]

     B. What is a palanquin?

     C. A litter.

  3 A. The matter may be compared with the case of a king who had an only daughter who was beautiful, pious, and gracious.

     B. Said the king to his staff, "my daughter is beautiful, pious, and gracious, and yet you do not make her a litter? Make her a litter, for it is better that the beauty of my daughter should appear from within a litter."

     C. So said the Holy One, blessed be he, "My Torah is beautiful, pious, and gracious, and yet you do not make an ark for it?

     D. "It is better that the beauty of my Torah should appear from within the ark."

Now we revert to our original program, and, as before, we show how the ark for the Torah, which was in the Temple, is what King Solomon made. We do this by citing verses of Exodus that speak of the ark.

4 A. [Reverting to 1.C:] " 'King Solomon made himself': the king to whom peace belongs."

B. " 'from the wood of Lebanon': 'And Bezalel made the ark of acacia-wood' " (Ex. 37:1).

C. " 'He made its posts of silver': these are the two pillars that stand within the ark, which were made of silver."

D. " 'its back of gold': 'and he overlaid it with pure gold' " (Ex. 37:2).

5 A. "its seat of purple":

B. Rabbi Tanhuma says, "This is the veil that adjoined it."

C. Rabbi Bibi said, "This refers to the ark cover, for the gold of the ark-cover was like purple."

We come to the third, the human component, of our metaphor. The role of "the daughters in Jerusalem" in regard to the ark of the Torah is the same as before. Then we have the expected footnote, No. 7, and a topical appendix added to provide information but not to advance the argument, No. 8.

6 A. "it was lovingly wrought within by the daughters of Jerusalem:"

B. Rabbi Yudah said, "This refers to the merit accruing to the Torah and those who study it."

C. Rabbi Azariah said in the name of Rabbi Yudah and in the name of Rabbi Simon, "This refers to the presence of God."

7 A. Said Rabbi Abba ben Kahana, " 'And there I will meet with you' " (Ex. 25:22):

B. "This serves to teach you that even what is on the other side of the ark cover, the space was not empty of the Presence of God."

8 A. A gentile asked Rabbi Joshua ben Qorha, "Why did the Holy One, blessed be he, speak from within the bush and not from any other tree?"

B. He said to him, "Had he spoke with him from the midst of a carob or a sycamore, you would have asked the same thing, and would I have had to answer you?"

C. "Nonetheless, to turn you away with nothing is
not possible."
D. "It serves to teach you that there is no place in
the world that is empty of the presence of God."
E. "For even from within the bush did he speak
with him."

The ark now takes its place, the natural next step after the tent
of meeting. The basic point is completed at No. 6, and the rest is
a secondary expansion on the general theme of the ark (how it
was made and so forth). We move from the Temple to the house
of the sanctuary within, going through the familiar repertoire. In
what follows there are no surprises, and by identifying the ampli-
fying materials and appendix inserts, we see how a disciplined
plan governs throughout.

XLIII:iii.1 A. [Supply: "King Solomon made himself a palan-
quin from the wood of Lebanon. He made its
posts of silver, its back of gold, its seat of purple;
it was lovingly wrought within by the daughters
of Jerusalem":]
B. Another interpretation of "a palanquin":
C. This refers to the house of the sanctuary.
D. "King Solomon made himself":
E. This refers in fact to Solomon.
F. "from the wood of Lebanon":
G. "And we will cut wood out of Lebanon" (2 Chr.
2:15).
H. "He made its posts of silver":
I. "And he set up the pillars of the porch of the
Temple" (1 Kgs. 7:21).
J. "its back of gold":
K. So we have learned on Tannaite authority: The
entire house was overlaid with gold, except the
backs of the doors.
L. Said Rabbi Isaac, "That teaching on Tannaite
authority applies to the second building, but as
to the first building, even the back parts of the
doors were covered with gold."

2 A. We have learned: Seven kinds of gold were in it: [Simon:] good gold, pure gold, chased gold, beaten gold, gold of *mufaz,* refined gold, gold of *parvayim.*

B. good gold: meant literally. "And the gold of that land is good" (Gen. 2:12).

C. In this regard Rabbi Isaac said, "It is good to have in the house, good to take on a trip."

D. pure gold: for they would put it into the furnace and come out undiminished.

E. Rabbi Judah in the name of Rabbi Ammi: "A thousand bars of gold did Solomon put into the furnace a thousand times, until they yielded a single bar."

F. But lo, said Rabbi Yosé ben Rabbi Judah on Tannaite authority, "There was the case that the candlestick of the Temple was heavier than that of the wilderness by the weight of one Gordian *denarius,* and it was passed through the furnace eighty times, until it lost the excess."

G. But to begin with it lost dross, and thereafter it lacked only the smallest volume.

H. beaten gold.

I. for it was drawn out like wax.

J. Hadrian had an egg's bulk of it.

K. Diocletian had a Gordian *denarius's* volume of it.

L. This government today has none of it and never had any of it.

M. chased gold: it bears that name because [Simon:] it made all the goldsmiths shut up their shops.

N. Lo, it is written, "Seven thousand talents of refined silver, with which to overlay the walls of the houses" (1 Chr. 29:4):

O. Was it silver? Was it not gold? And why call it silver?

P. It was to shame everyone who owned gold.

Q. And from it were made all of the utensils, the basins, pots, shovels, snuffers, bowls, forks, spoons, censers, and *potot.*

R. Rabbi Isaac of Magdala said, " '*Potot*' are pivots."

S. Rabbi Sima said, "It refers to a cup under the hinge."

T. This teaches you that the sanctuary was not lacking even the most minor thing.

U. gold of *mufaz:*

V. Rabbi Patriqi, brother of Rabbi Derosah in the name of Rabbi Abba ben Rabbi Bunah said, "It was like sulphur flaring up in the fire."

W. Rabbi Abun said, "It is so called by reason of the country in which it originates, which is Ufaz."

X. refined gold:

Y. The household of Rabbi Yannai and the household of Rabbi Yudan ben Rabbi Simeon:

Z. The household of Rabbi Yannai said, "They cut it into the size of olives and feed it to ostriches, and they defecate it in refined condition."

AA. The household of Rabbi Yudan ben Rabbi Simeon said, "They buried it in dung for seven years and it would come out refined."

BB. gold of *paravayim:*

CC. Rabbi Simeon ben Laqish said, "It was red, like the blood of a bullock."

DD. Some say, "It produces fruit."

EE. For when Solomon built the house of the sanctuary, he made with it every kind of tree, and when the trees produced fruit, the ones in the Temple did too, and the fruit would drop from the trees and be gathered and was saved for the upkeep of the Temple.

FF. But when Manasseh set up an idol in the Temple, all the trees withered: "And the flower of Lebanon languishes" (Nah. 1:4).

GG. But in the age to come, the Holy One, blessed be he, will bring them back: "It shall blossom abundantly and rejoice, even with joy and singing" (Is. 35:2).

3 A. "its seat of purple":

B. "And he made the veil of blue and purple and crimson and fine linen" (2 Chr. 3:14).

4 A. "it was lovingly wrought within by the daughters of Jerusalem":

B. Rabbi Yudan said, "This refers to the merit attained through the Torah and the merit attained through the righteous who occupy themselves with it."

C. Rabbi Azariah in the name of Rabbi Judah in the name of Rabbi Simon said, "This refers to the presence of God."

From the ark, we move on to the sanctuary, with predictable results. The object chosen as metaphor is primary; the expansion of the verses that are used to amplify the connection is secondary. That the framers have nothing new to say once they have selected their basic object for metaphorization is shown at the end, which is repeated verbatim. That shows that the motivation derives not from the base-verse but from the basic plan.

Now comes the surprise, except for those who realize that for our sages the Temple always represents the world of creation, heaven and earth together. That is the point of the penultimate metaphor, building to a climax and forming a critical step in our progress. The Temple that Solomon made refers to the world, and we shall now see how we are able to read our base-verse in such a light on the basis of verses of scripture.

XLIII:iv.1 A. [Supply: "King Solomon made himself a palanquin from the wood of Lebanon. He made its posts of silver, its back of gold, its seat of purple; it was lovingly wrought within by the daughters of Jerusalem":]

B. Another interpretation of "a palanquin:"

C. This refers to the world.

D. "King Solomon made himself":

E. the king to whom peace belongs.

F. "from the wood of Lebanon":

G. for [the world] was built out of the house of the Most Holy Place down below.

2 A. For we have learned on Tannaite authority:

B. When the ark was removed [after 586 B.C.E.], a stone remained there from the days of the earlier prophets, called foundation stone [*shetiyyah*].

    C. Why was it called foundation stone [*shetiyyah*]?

    D. For upon it the world was based [the word *based* uses the same consonants as the word for foundation, *shetiyyah*].

    E. That is in line with this verse: "Out of Zion, the perfection of beauty, God has shined forth" (Ps. 50:2).

3 A. "He made its posts of silver":

    B. This refers to the chain of genealogies.

    C. "its back of gold":

    D. This speaks of the produce of the earth and of the tree, which are exchanged for gold.

    E. "its seat of purple":

    F. "Who rides upon heaven as your help" (Dt. 33:26).

    N. "it was lovingly wrought within by the daughters of Jerusalem":

    O. Rabbi Yudah said, "This refers to the merit attained through the Torah and the merit attained through the righteous who occupy themselves with it."

    P. Rabbi Azariah in the name of Rabbi Judah and in the name of Rabbi Simon said, "This refers to the presence of God."

It is not a surprising move from the Temple to the natural world, since the Temple and its cult are understood to correspond to the world beyond the walls, which focuses within. There the produce of nature is offered to the supernatural. So the symbolism proceeds on a steady course and its goal is now introduced, for the next move is from this world upward to God. We move from start to finish on a single, straight path, from the Israelite in his prayer garments speaking prayers upward to Heaven, through the Temple and its sanctuary, onward thence to the heavens above, and now to the heights of the heavens where God is enthroned.

XLIII:v.1 A. [Supply: "King Solomon made himself a palanquin from the wood of Lebanon. He made its

posts of silver, its back of gold, its seat of purple;
it was lovingly wrought within by the daughters
of Jerusalem":]

B. Another interpretation of "a palanquin":
C. This refers to the throne of glory.
D. "King Solomon made himself":
E. the king to whom peace belongs.
F. "from the wood of Lebanon":
G. This is the House of the Most Holy Place above,
which is directly opposite the House of the Most
Holy Place down below,
H. as in the following usage: "The place . . . for you
to dwell in" (Ex. 15:17),
I. that is, directly opposite your dwelling place
[above].
J. "He made its posts of silver":
K. "The pillars of heaven tremble" (Job 26:11).
L. "its back of gold":
M. This refers to teachings of the Torah: "More to
be desired are they than gold, yes, than much
fine gold" (Ps. 19:11).
N. "its seat of purple":
O. "To him who rides upon the heaven of heavens,
which are of old" (Ps. 68:34).
P. "it was lovingly wrought within by the daugh-
ters of Jerusalem."

To be consistent with what I have already said, I am con-
strained to identify what follows in the form of a footnote. But in
fact, we see, the content of this "appended" item serves as the climax and conclusion of the whole, the final lines spelling out the
message of the entire, rich metaphorical statement that has gone
before.

Q. Rabbi Berekhiah and Rabbi Bun in the name
of Rabbi Abbahu: "There are four proud
[creatures]":
R. "The pride of birds is the eagle."
S. "The pride of domesticated beasts is the ox."
T. "The pride of wild beasts is the lion."

U. "The pride of them all is man."

V. "And all of them did the Holy One, blessed be he, take and engrave on the throne of glory: 'The Lord has established his throne in the heavens and his kingdom rules over all' (Ps. 103: 19).

W. "Because 'The Lord has established his throne in the heavens,' therefore: 'his kingdom rules over all.' "

The conclusion is truly triumphant, as we now succeed in holding together earth with Heaven within the single metaphor. The palanquin has stood for each of the principal components of the world of sanctification in nature, cult, and the supernatural. All is made explicit. The love, then, is cosmopolitan: King Solomon's palanquin is all of reality, which loves, and is loved by, God.

6

Song of Songs Rabbah to Song of Songs 4:1

Behold, you are beautiful, my love,
behold you are beautiful!
Your eyes are doves behind your veil.
Your hair is like a flock of goats
moving down the slopes of Gilead.

Lest you think that when our sages sought for metaphors of God's love, they turned only to what was public, the life of Israel in prayer, the Temple, the sea, and Sinai, we turn to a range of metaphors drawn from everyday life: the life of do this, don't do that, that the observant Jew is directed by the Torah to live. The litany that follows simply identifies the beauty marks to which "behold, you are beautiful, my love" makes reference. These are a long list of deeds from the general to the specific. The general begins with "religious deeds," that is, performance of the commandments *(mitzvot);* then, beyond what is commanded, what cannot be commanded but can only be done as an act of undemanded grace, the love that cannot be commanded by is performed by the Jew who loves God. This is followed at 1.D and E, by final generalizations, referring to commandments that require affirmative actions and those that require refraining from certain deeds. The former would be typified by the commandment to recite the Shema morning and night, the latter by the commandment not to eat unkosher food.

What follows is a long list of specific deeds of home and field, clothing, planting and harvest, circumcision, and on and on. By this point, readers will not be surprised by the freedom of our sages in identifying appropriate metaphors for Israel's beauty marks. Nor are these only what some call "external," since, in the flow of the list, we come to marks of spirituality such as repentence of sin, doing good deeds with the right attitude, and belief in the correspondence of the life in this world and the life in the world to come. It would be difficult to find a more encompassing or authoritative account of the entire theology of Judaism in a single catalogue of entries, each of which exposes a fresh trait of the life of consecration to God.

XLV:i.1   A. "Behold, you are beautiful, my love, behold you are beautiful":

        B. "Behold you are beautiful" in religious deeds,

        C. "Behold you are beautiful" in acts of grace,

        D. "Behold you are beautiful" in carrying out religious obligations of commission,

        E. "Behold you are beautiful" in carrying out religious obligations of omission,

        F. "Behold you are beautiful" in carrying out the religious duties of the home, in separating priestly ration and tithes,

        G. "Behold you arc beautiful" in carrying out the religious duties of the field, gleanings, forgotten sheaves, the corner of the field, poor person's tithe, and declaring the field ownerless.

        H. "Behold you are beautiful" in observing the taboo against mixed species.

        I. "Behold you are beautiful" in providing a linen cloak with woolen show-fringes.

        J. "Behold you are beautiful" in [keeping the rules governing] planting,

        K. "Behold you are beautiful" in keeping the taboo on uncircumcised produce,

        L. "Behold you are beautiful" in keeping the laws on produce in the fourth year after the planting of an orchard,

        M. "Behold you are beautiful" in circumcision,

    N. "Behold you are beautiful" in trimming the wound,

    O. "Behold you are beautiful" in reciting the Prayer,

    P. "Behold you are beautiful" in reciting the Shema,

    Q. "Behold you are beautiful" in putting a mezuzah on the doorpost of your house,

    R. "Behold you are beautiful" in wearing phylacteries,

    S. "Behold you are beautiful" in building the tabernacle for the Festival of Tabernacles,

    T. "Behold you are beautiful" in taking the palm branch and etrog on the Festival of Tabernacles,

    U. "Behold you are beautiful" in repentance,

    V. "Behold you are beautiful" in good deeds,

    W. "Behold you are beautiful" in this world,

    X. "Behold you are beautiful" in the world to come.

We should not suppose that the entire document is made up of these lists. Here is a case in which the list gives way to a phrase by phrase amplification of that to which a verse or clause makes reference, that is to say, "commentary" in a more conventional sense. We want to know what "your eyes are doves" means. We propose a hypothesis, B, and then introduce a prooftext, C.

  2 A. "your eyes are doves":

    B. "your eyes" stand for the Sanhedrin, which is the eyesight of the community.

    C. That is in line with this verse: "If it is hid from the eyes of the community" (Num. 15:24).

    D. There are two hundred forty-eight limbs in a human being, and all of them function only through eyesight.

    E. So the Israelites can function only in line with their Sanhedrin.

The same program continues at No. 3. We ask what the metaphor, "doves," stands for, or why Israel is compared to "doves," as our base-verse does. The meanings then flow from the nature of the dove.

3 A. "doves":
   B. Just as a dove is innocent, so the Israelites are [Simon supplies: innocent; just as the dove is beautiful in its movement, so Israelites are] beautiful in their movement, when they go up for the pilgram festivals.
   C. Just as a dove is distinguished, so the Israelites are distinguished: in not shaving, in circumcision, in wearing show-fringes.
   D. Just as the dove is modest, so the Israelites are modest.
   E. Just as the dove puts forth its neck for slaughter, so the Israelites: "For your sake are we killed all day long" (Ps. 44:23).
   F. Just as the dove atones for sin, so the Israelites atone for other nations,
   G. For all those seventy bullocks that they offer on the Festival of Tabernacles correspond to the nations of the world, so that the world should not become desolate on their account: "In return for my love they are my adversaries, but I am all prayer" (Ps. 109:4).
   H. Just as the dove, once it recognizes its mate, never again changes him for another, so the Israelites, once they recognized the Holy One, blessed be he, never exchanged him for another.
   I. Just as the dove, when it enters its nest, recognizes its nest and young, fledglings and apertures, so the three rows of the disciples of the sages, when they take their seats before them, knows each one his place.
   J. Just as the dove, even though you take its fledglings from under it, does not ever abandon its cote, so the Israelites, even though the house of the sanctuary was destroyed, never nullified the three annual pilgrim festivals.
   K. Just as the dove renews its brood month by month, so the Israelites every month renew Torah and good deeds.
   L. Just as the dove [Simon:] goes far afield but re-

turns to her cote, so do the Israelites: "They shall come trembling as a bird out of Egypt" (Hos. 11:11): this speaks of the generation of the wilderness. "And as a dove out of the land of Assyria" (Hos. 11:11); this speaks of the Ten Tribes.

M. And in both cases: "And I will make them dwell in their houses, says the Lord" (Hos. 11:11).

Now we realize that a powerful message emerges not only through a catalogue of holy things, but also through the exposition of a metaphor. I see no important element of the entire faith of the Torah that is omitted in the metaphor, "Israel is like a dove," that is, "Your eyes are doves behind your veil" yields a stunning set of propositions. But each of these can have been reduced to an entry on a list. The upshot is, whichever way we turn, our reading of Song of Songs remains an utterly theological interpretation in which the whole of the faith is located in each and every detail of the poem, just as we claimed at the very outset. We note now an appendix of thematically pertinent materials, which do not contribute in any way to the foregoing.

4 A. Rabbi says, "There is a kind of dove, who, when it is being fed, attracts her fellows, who smell her scent and come to her cote.

B. "So when an elder is in session and expounding, many proselytes convert at that time, for example, Jethro, who heard and came, and Rahab, who heard and came.

C. "Likewise on account of Hananiah, Mishael, and Azariah, many converted: 'For when he sees his children . . . sanctify my name . . . they also that err in spirit shall come to understanding'" (Is. 29:23).

5 A. Rabbi was in session and expounding, but the community's attention wandered, so he wanted to wake them up. He said, "A single woman in Egypt produced six hundred thousand at a single birth."

B. Now there was present a disciple, named Rabbi

Ishmael ben Rabbi Yosé, who said to him, "Who was this?"

C. He said to him, "This was Jochebed, who produced Moses, and he was numbered as the equal to six hundred thousand Israelites: 'Then sang Moses and the children of Israel' (Ex. 15:1); 'And the children of Israel did according to all that the Lord has commanded Moses' (Num. 1:54); 'And there has not arisen a prophet in Israel like Moses'" (Dt. 34:10).

The metaphor moves onward; No. 6 contains only one surprise, and that is the allusion for Noah. An appendix is tacked on.

6 A. "your eyes are doves":

B. They are like doves.

C. Your likeness is similar to that of the dove:

D. Just as a dove brought light to the world, so you bring light to the world: "And nations shall walk at your light" (Is. 60:3).

E. When did a dove bring light to the world?

F. In the time of Noah: "And the dove came in to him in the evening, and lo, in her mouth was an olive leaf, freshly plucked" (Gen. 8:11).

7 A. [Supply: "And the dove came in to him in the evening, and lo, in her mouth was an olive leaf, freshly plucked" (Gen. 8:11):] What is the meaning of "freshly plucked"?

B. It was killed: "Joseph is without doubt torn in pieces" (Gen. 37:33).

C. Said Rabbi Berekhiah, "Had she not killed it, it would have turned into a great tree."

8 [= Genesis Rabbah XXX:vi.3:] A. Whence did the dove bring the olive branch?

B. Rabbi Levi [Gen. R.: Abba] said, "She brought it from the young shoots in the Land of Israel."

C. [Gen. R.: Rabbi Levi said, "She brought it from the mount of Olives,] for the Land of Israel had not been submerged in the flood. That is in line with what the Holy One, blessed be he, said to

Ezekiel, 'Son of man, say to her: "You are a land that is not cleaned nor rained upon in the day of indignation"' (Ez. 22:24).

D. Rabbi Yohanan said, "Even millstone cases dissolved in the water of the flood."

E. Rabbi Tarye [Gen. R.: Birai] said, "The gates of the garden of Eden opened for the dove, and from there she brought it."

F. Said to him Rabbi Abbahu, "If she had brought it from the garden of Eden, should the dove not have brought something of greater value, such as cinnamon or balsam? But in choosing the olive leaf, the dove gave a signal to Noah, saying to him, 'Noah, better is something bitter from this [source, namely,] the Holy One, blessed be he, than something sweet from you.'"

The pattern of No. 1 derives from the hermeneutic that treats our poem as a source of metaphors for Israel's religious reality. No. 2 follows suit. No. 3 reverts to the metaphor of the dove for Israel. No. 4 is attached with good reason, and No. 5 is parachuted down because it was attached to No. 4 before No. 4 entered our document; the principle of agglutination prior to the making of documents clearly was the making of collections in the names of authorities. No. 6 then reverts to our base-verse, and it also introduces the inevitable appearance of the dove in the story of Noah. The rest then is attached for thematic reasons.

7

Song of Songs Rabbah to Song of Songs 8:1

O that you were like a brother to me,
that nursed at my mother's breast!
If I met you outside, I would kiss you,
and none would despise me.

Reading the whole of Israel's history as genealogy, and the entirety of the family's genealogy as present in the here and now, our sages proceed to a reading somewhat different from those we have seen. Here we simply answer the question, to what in our family does the Song make reference? And then we review a range of candidates for that "brother" who would be the one God has in mind in speaking of Israel's relationship to God. So the relationships within a family are turned into metaphors for God's and Israel's union.

CIII:i.1 A. "O that you were like a brother to me":
          B. Like what sort of brother?
          C. Like Cain with Abel? Cain killed Abel: "Cain rose up against his brother Abel and slew him" (Gen. 4:8).
          D. Like Ishmael with Isaac? Ishmael hated Isaac.
          E. Like Esau and Jacob?

F. Lo, it is said, "And Esau hated Jacob" (Gen. 27:41).

G. Like the brothers of Joseph with Joseph? They hated him: "And his brothers envied him" (Gen. 37:11).

H. Then like what brother? It is one "that nursed at my mother's breast," namely, Joseph with Benjamin, who loved him with all his heart. "And when Joseph saw Benjamin with them" (Gen. 43:16).

2 A. "If I met you outside, I would kiss you":

B. "outside": this refers to the wilderness, which is outside the settled territory.

C. "I would kiss you":

D. through the two brothers who kissed one another, Moses and Aaron: "And he went and met him in the mountain of God and kissed him" (Ex. 4:27).

3 A. "and none would despise me":

B. Said Rabbi Phineas, "There was the case of two brothers, one in Meron, the other in Gush Halab. A fire burned up the house of the one who was in Meron. His sister came from Gush Halab and began to hug and embrace and kiss him, saying to him, 'This [public embrace] does not make me despicable, because my brother was in great danger, from which he has been saved.'"

The comments now begin away from the Song as narrow-based exegesis: which brother is meant? But the reference point is consistent with the principal line of interpretation—Israel in the time of the patriarchs, Israel in Egypt—and that of course supplies the point of interest. The point of No. 3 is that the embrace of God and Israel—when God finds Israel in the wilderness—is not to be despised, because God will rejoice as a sister rejoices for her brother who has been saved from danger.

8

Song of Songs Rabbah to Song of Songs 8:6

Set me as a seal upon your heart,
as a seal upon your arm; for love is
strong as death, jealousy is cruel as
the grave. Its flashes are flashes of fire,
a most vehement flame.

From the outward life of faith, we proceed inward to the relationship of emotion and sentiment. Here is where the life with God is lived, as much as in the expressions of piety that in outer form give expression to inner attitudes of love, loyalty, and faithfulness. Naked emotion, not only that which is garbed in the form of gesture or language, is addressed in our base-verse concerning love and jealousy. These most primal emotions on their own terms speak of God's and Israel's feelings for one another. God loves Israel unto death, but Israel makes God jealous with its idolatry. Isaac loved Esau unto death, but Esau was jealous of Jacob. Jacob loved Joseph unto death, but the brothers were jealous of him—and so on through the repertoire. The climax comes with the love of husband and wife. God is the husband, Israel, the wife; God loves Israel unto death, but Israel makes God jealous.

CVIII:ii.1　A. "for love is strong as death":

　　B. As strong as death is the love with which the

Holy One, blessed be he, loves Israel: "I have loved you says the Lord" (Mal. 1:2).

C. "jealousy is cruel as the grave":

D. That is when they make him jealous with their idolatry: "They roused him to jealousy with strange gods" (Dt. 32:16).

2 A. Another explanation of "for love is strong as death":

B. As strong as death is the love with which Isaac loved Esau: "Now Isaac loved Esau" (Gen. 25:28).

C. "jealousy is cruel as the grave":

D. The jealousy that Esau held against Jacob: "And Esau hated Jacob" (Gen. 27:41).

3 A. Another explanation of "for love is strong as death":

B. As strong as death is the love with which Jacob loved Joseph: "Now Israel loved Joseph more than all his children" (Gen. 37:3).

C. "jealousy is cruel as the grave":

D. The jealousy that his brothers held against him: "And his brothers envied him" (Gen. 37:11).

4 A. Another explanation of "for love is strong as death":

B. As strong as death is the love with which Jonathan loved David: "And Jonathan loved him as his own soul" (1 Sam. 18:1).

C. "jealousy is cruel as the grave":

D. The jealousy of Saul against David: "And Saul eyed David" (1 Sam. 18:9).

5 A. Another explanation of "for love is strong as death":

B. As strong as death is the love with which a man loves his wife: "Enjoy life with the wife whom you love" (Qoh. 9:9).

C. "jealousy is cruel as the grave":

D. The jealousy that she causes in him and leads him to say to her, "Do not speak with such-and-so."

E. If she goes and speaks with that man, forthwith: "The spirit of jealousy comes upon him and he is jealous on account of his wife" (Num. 5:14).

6 A. Another explanation of "for love is strong as death":

   B. As strong as death is the love with which the generation that suffered the repression loved the Holy One, blessed be he: "No, but for your sake we are killed all day long" (Ps. 44:23).

   C. "jealousy is cruel as the grave":

   D. The jealousy that the Holy One, blessed be he, will hold for Zion, that is a great zealousness: "Thus says the Lord, I am jealous for Zion with a great jealousy" (Zech. 1:14).

7 A. "Its flashes are flashes of fire, a most vehement flame":

   B. Rabbi Berekiah said, "Like the fire that is on high,"

   C. "that fire does not consume water, nor water, fire."

The exposition, Nos. 1–6, shows us a satisfying way in which to put together and amplify a base-verse. We are able to encompass a variety of topics, yet both formally and conceptually make a coherent statement. We contrast love and jealousy, favoring the one, denigrating the other. No. 1 does not prepare us for that contrast, since here God's love for Israel contrasts with the emotions that Israel provokes in God; yet the contrast is established, so the rest will follow. No. 2, Isaac, Jacob, and Esau, No. 3, Jacob, Joseph, and the brothers, No. 4, Jonathan, David, and Saul, No. 5, man, wife, and paramour—all then work in sets of three, and No. 6 reverts to the pattern of No. 1. Aesthetically this must be considered a perfect design, one without a single false move. No. 7 is routine.

9

Song of Songs Rabbah to Song of Songs 8:8–10

*We have a little sister, and she has
no breasts. What shall we do for
our sister, on the day when she is
spoken for? (8:8) If she is a wall,
we will build upon her a battlement
of silver; but if she is a door,
we will enclose her with boards
of cedar. (8:9) I was a wall,
and my breasts were like towers;
then I was in his eyes
as one who brings peace. (8:10)*

Until now, the history of holy Israel has figured only at fixed
points—the sea, Sinai, the Temple, and the like. But how about
the movement of Israel through time—its pilgrim's progress to
the peace of God? In our reading of the verse at hand—not a
likely candidate for re-visioning in terms of the story of the holy
people—we rehearse the great events from start to finish. Where
previously the tableaux had been stationary; now we see a stage
with action. We start with the event of Abraham, that is, reading
the life of the beginning of Israel in line with our base-verse.

CX:i.2   A. Rabbi Berekhiah interpreted the verse to speak
            of our father, Abraham:
          B. " 'We have a little sister': this refers to Abraham,
            as it is said, 'Abraham was one and he inherited
            the land' " (Ezr. 33:24).

C. "[The sense is,] he stitched together all those who pass through the world before the Holy One, blessed be he [since the word for one and stitched together share the same consonants]."

D. Bar Qappara said, "He was like a man who stitches a tear."

E. [Continuing C:] "While he was still a child, he engaged in religious duties and good deeds."

F. "and she has no breasts": he had not yet reached the age at which he was subject to the obligation of carrying out religious duties and good deeds.

G. " 'What shall we do for our sister, on the day when she is spoken for?': On the day on which the wicked Nimrod made a decree and told him to go down into the fiery furnace."

CXI:i.1   A. [Continuing CX:i.2:] "If she is a wall, we will build upon her a battlement of silver":

B. "If she is a wall": this refers to Abraham.

C. Said the Holy One, blessed be he, "If he insists on his views like a firm wall,"

D. "We will build upon her a battlement of silver": we shall save him and build him in the world.

E. "But if she is a door": if he is poor [a word that uses consonants that appear also in the word for door], impoverished of religious duties and [Simon:] sways to and fro in his conduct like a door,

F. " 'We will enclose her with boards of cedar': just as a drawing [a word that uses the same consonants as the word for enclose] lasts for only a brief hour, so I will stand over him for only a brief time. [Simon, p. 312, n. 2: In his own lifetime only, but his merit will not be so great that I should stand by his children for his sake.]"

G. Said Abraham before the Holy One, blessed be he, " 'I was a wall: and I shall be insistent upon my habit of doing good deeds like a firm wall.' "

H. " 'and my breasts were like towers': for I am destined to raise up parties and fellowships of righteous men in my model in your world."

I. "Then I was in his eyes as one who brings peace":

J. Said to him the Holy One, blessed be he, "Just as you descended into the fiery furnace, so I shall bring you out in peace: 'I am the Lord who brought you out of the furnace of the Chaldeans'" (Gen. 15:7).

The first reading of the verse is fully worked out, with enormous care as to matching details, and the metaphor of the little sister has God praise Abraham. We proceed to a quite separate reading of the same metaphor. I see no interpolated material, only a sustained and well-crafted exposition of one thing in terms of something else, beautifully articulated. Now from Abraham, the next stop of Sodom and Israel, we see the contrast between the earthly and the heavenly city.

CXI:ii.1   A. Rabbi Yohanan interpreted the verses to speak of Sodom and of Israel:

B. "'We have a little sister': this refers to Sodom. 'And your elder sister is Samaria ... and your younger sister ... is Sodom'" (Ezr. 16:46).

C. "'and she has no breasts': for she has not sucked of the milk of religious duties and good deeds" [by contrast to Abraham].

D. "'What shall we do for our sister, on the day when she is spoken for?': on the day on which the heavenly court made the decree that she is to be burned in fire. 'Then the Lord caused to rain upon Sodom and upon Gomorrah brimstone and fire'" (Gen. 19:24).

E. "'If she is a wall, we will build upon her a battlement of silver'": this refers to Israel.

F. "Said the Holy One, blessed be he, 'If they stand firm in their good deeds like a wall, "we will build upon them" and deliver them.'"

G. "'But if she is a door': if they [Simon] sway to and fro in their conduct like a door,"

H. "'we will enclose her with boards of cedar': [God continues] 'just as a drawing lasts for only a brief hour, so I will stand over him for only a brief time.' "

I. " 'I was a wall': said the Israelites before the Holy One, blessed be he, 'Lord of the world, we are a wall, and we shall stand by the religious duties and good deeds [that we practice] as firm as a wall.' "

J. " 'and my breasts were like towers': 'for we are destined to raise up parties and fellowships of righteous men in my model in your world.' "

K. " 'Then I was in his eyes as one who brings peace': Why so? For all the nations of the world taunt Israel, saying to them, 'If so, why has he sent you into exile from his land, and why has he destroyed his sanctuary?' "

L. "And the Israelites reply to them, 'We are like a princess who went to celebrate in her father's house the [Simon:] first wedding anniversary after her marriage.' [That is why we are in exile in Babylonia.]"

Now that we have introduced the theme of Israel and the nations, we move directly to another confrontation between Israel and the nations, besides the one at Sodom. It is now the nation's effort to force Israel to betray God and abandon the holy way of life of religious duties and good deeds. For this reading, the metaphor invoked involves Hananiah, Mishael, and Azariah.

2 A. Another interpretation of "If she is a wall":

B. This refers to Hananiah, Mishael, and Azariah.

C. Said the Holy One, blessed be he, "If they stand firm in their good deeds like a wall, 'we will build upon them' and deliver them."

D. " 'but if she is a door' ": if they sway to and fro in their conduct like a door,

E. " 'we will enclose her with boards of cedar': [God continues] just as a drawing lasts for only a brief hour, so I will stand over them for only a brief time."

F. "I was a wall": said they before the Holy One,

blessed be he, "[Lord of the world,] we are a wall, and we shall stand by the religious duties and good deeds [that we practice] as firm as a wall."

G. " 'and my breasts were like towers': for we are destined to raise up parties and fellowships of righteous men in my model in your world."

H. "Then I was in his eyes as one who brings peace":

I. Said to them the Holy One, blessed be he, "Just as you have gone down into the fiery furnace in peace, so I shall bring you out of there in peace: 'Then Shadrach, Meshach, and Abednego came forth' " (Dan. 3:26).

We see now how carefully matched the treatments of the base-verses are. The possibility of understanding 1.L, in particular, derives solely from the initial reading in terms of Abraham. That seems to me the point of the exercise, thus far: to link Israel's exile to Babylonia to Abraham's initial origin. Not only so, but the link between Abraham in the fiery furnace and Shadrach, Meshach, and Abednego is explicit. That proves beyond a doubt the unity of the "another interpretation," and shows that the whole was planned as a single composition to express one fundamental and encompassing point. The third and final exposition, which completes the set, confirms that view. From the Babylonian exile, in which the three saints figure, we proceed to the return to the land of Israel, at which point, in the sacred history of Israel, the movement of Israel's history should come to an end, and a permanent, and perfect, stasis should take effect.

CXI:iii.1 A. Rabbis interpret the verses to speak of those who came up from the exile:

B. " 'We have a little sister' ": this refers to those who came up from the Exile.

C. "little": because they were few in numbers.

D. "and she has no breasts": this refers to the five matters in which the second house [Temple] was less than the first one:

E. "(1) fire from above, (2) anointing oil, (3) the

ark, (4) the Holy Spirit, and (5) access to the Urim and Thumim: 'And I will take pleasure in it and I will be glorified says the Lord' (Hag. 1:8), with the word for 'I will be glorified' written without the letter H, which stands for five."

F. " 'What shall we do for our sister, on the day when she is spoken for': On the day on which Cyrus issues the decree, 'Whoever has crossed the Euphrates has crossed, but whoever has not crossed will not cross.' "

G. " 'If she is a wall': if the Israelites had gone up like a wall from Babylonia, the house of the sanctuary that they built at that time would not have been destroyed a second time [a sufficiently large population having been able to defend it]."

2 A. Rabbi Zeira went out to the market to buy things and said to the storekeeper, "Weigh carefully."

B. He said to him, "Why don't you get out of here, Babylonian, whose fathers destroyed the Temple!"

C. Then Rabbi Zeira said, "Are my fathers not the same as that man's fathers?"

D. He went into the meeting house and heard Rabbi Shila's voice in session, expounding, " 'If she is a wall': if the Israelites had gone up like a wall from Babylonia, the house of the sanctuary that they built at that time would not have been destroyed a second time."

E. He said, "Well did that ignoramus teach me."

3 A. [Reverting to 1.G:] " 'but if she is a door, we will enclose her with boards of cedar' ": just as in the case of a drawing, if it is removed, still its traces are to be discerned,

B. "So even though the house of the sanctuary has been destroyed, the Israelites have not annulled their pilgrim festivals three times a year."

C. "I was a wall":

D. Said Rabbi Aibu, "Said the Holy One, blessed be

he, 'I am going to make an advocate for Israel among the nations of the world.' "

E. "And what is it? It is the echo: 'Except the Lord of hosts had left to us a very small remnant' " (Is. 1:9).

4 A. It has been taught on Tannaite authority:

B. Once the final prophets, Haggai, Zechariah, and Malachi had died, the Holy Spirit ceased from Israel.

C. Even so, they would make use of the echo.

5 A. There was the case of sages voting in the upper room of the house of Gedia in Jericho. An echo came forth and said to them, "There is among you one man who is worthy of receiving the Holy Spirit, but his generation is not suitable for such to happen."

B. They set their eyes upon Hillel the Elder.

C. When he died, they said in his regard, "Woe for the modest one, woe for the pious one, the disciple of Ezra."

6 A. There was another case, in which the Israelite sages took a vote, in the vineyard in Yavneh.

B. Now were they really *in* a vineyard? Rather, [they were like a vineyard, for] this was the Sanhedrin, that sat in rows and rows, lines and lines, like a well-ordered vineyard.

C. An echo came forth and said to them, "There is among you one man who is worthy of receiving the Holy Spirit, but his generation is not suitable for such to happen."

D. They set their eyes upon Samuel the Younger.

E. When he died, they said in his regard, "Woe for the modest one, woe for the pious one, the disciple of Hillel the Elder."

7 A. Also: he said three things when he was dying: "Simeon and Ishmael are for the sword, the rest of his colleagues are destined to be killed, the rest of the people to be plundered, and great sufferings are going to come upon the world."

B. This he said in Aramaic.

8 A. Also: for Judah ben Baba they ordained that when he died, they should say of him, "Woe for the modest one, woe for the pious one, the disciple of Samuel,"

B. But the time was inappropriate, for people do not conduct public funeral services for mourning for those put to death by the government.

9 A. There was the case in which Yohanan, the high priest, heard an echo come forth from the Most Holy Place, saying, "The young men who went out to war have won at Antioch."

B. They wrote down that day and that hour, and that is how matters were: on that very day they had won their victory.

10 A. There was the case in which Simeon the Righteous heard an echo come forth from the Most Holy Place, saying, "The action has been annulled that the enemy has planned to destroy the Temple, and Caius Caligula has been killed and his decrees annulled."

B. This he heard in Aramaic.

11 A. [Explaining the difference between the echo and the Holy Spirit or prophecy,] Rabbi Hunia in the name of Rabbi Reuben: "When the king is in town, people appeal to him and he acts."

B. "If the king is not in town, his icon is there."

C. "But the icon does not act in the way that the king can act."

12 A. Rabbi Yohanan and Rabbi Samuel ben Rabbi Nahman:

B. Rabbi Yohanan said, " 'But the Lord will give you there a trembling heart' " (Dt. 18:65):

C. "When they went up from exile, trembling, having been given to them, went up with them."

D. Rabbi Samuel ben Rabbi Nahman said, "There [in Babylonia] was trembling, but when they went up, they were healed."

13 A. When Rabbi Simeon ben Laqish saw them [Babylonians] swarming in the marketplace [in the

land of Israel], he would say to them, "Scatter yourselves."

B. He would say to them, "When you went up, you did not come up as a wall [of people 1.G], now have you come to form a wall [of people]?"

14 A. When Rabbi Yohanan would see them, he would rebuke them, saying, "If a prophet can rebuke them, 'My God will cast them away, because they did not listen to him' " (Hos. 9:17),

B. "Can I not rebuke them?"

15 A. Said Rabbi Abba ben Rabbi Kahana, "If you have seen the benches in the land of Israel filled with Babylonians, look forward for the coming of the Messiah."

B. "How come? 'He has spread a net for my feet' (Lam. 1:13). [The word for net has consonants shared with the word for Persians (see Simon, p. 317, n. 1, 'The presence of Babylonians (Persians) is a net to draw the Messiah').]"

16 A. Rabbi Simeon ben Yohai taught on Tannaite authority, "If you have seen a Persian horse tied up to gravestones in the land of Israel, look forward to the footsteps of the Messiah."

B. "How come? 'And this shall be peace: when the Assyrian shall come into our land, and when he shall tread in our palaces, then shall we raise against him seven shepherds and eight princes among men' " (Mic. 5:4).

17 A. [Supply: "And this shall be peace: when the Assyrian shall come into our land, and when he shall tread in our palaces, then shall we raise against him seven shepherds":]

B. Who are the seven shepherds?

C. David in the middle; to the right, Adam, Seth, and Methuselah; to the left, Abraham, Jacob, and Moses.

D. Where is Isaac? He takes a seat at the gate of Gehenna to deliver his descendants from the punishment of Gehenna.

E. "and eight princes among men":

F. Who are the eight princes?

G. Jesse, Saul, Samuel, Amos, Zephaniah, Heze-
kiah, Elijah, and the Messiah.

The final exposition reverts to the Babylonian exile, with reference to the return to Zion—hence Nos. 1 and 3, with a minor
interpolation at No. 2. The main point of the whole then cannot
be missed. The history of Israel from Abraham to the exile and
back to the land of Israel, encompassing also the Israelites in
the land of Israel after the destruction of the Second Temple, is
shown, and, ultimately, the resolution of the tension lies in Israel's access to continuing divine revelation through the heavenly
echo. How this fits with the allegation that in the Second Temple
there was no Holy Spirit is quite clear, and, in context, is an effec-
tive statement: the Holy Spirit, Urim and Thummim, and other
means of access to heaven have now been succeeded by the echo.
That, and one other consideration, accounts for tacking on the
heavenly echo materials that follow. The other consideration is
that Hillel came from Babylon—based on the materials available
to them, so our compilers believed. As is made explicit here, Hillel was a disciple of Ezra, in that he came from Babylonia to the
land of Israel and brought with him the Torah, just as Ezra had.
So the inclusion is not an accident and not a mere secondary expansion for essentially agglutinative reasons. It is deliberate and
further enriches the compilers' program and plan for this cogent
statement of theirs. Far be it from me to say that this is the best
of all possible Midrash-executions; but it surely sets a high standard for those to follow.

10

Symbol and Theology in Judaism

Since I maintain that our sages in Song of Songs Rabbah have read the Song of Songs as a sequence of symbols in verbal form, it is time to address the generalizations about theology and theological reading of scripture that I draw from what I represent as a sublime reading of scripture by the Torah sages. Precisely what do I mean by "symbol," and how do I know that a sign or cognitive representation, whether verbal or artistic, is symbolic? An ostensive definition suffices for the purpose of this book, which does not pretend to make a contribution of any kind to the theoretical literature of symbolism. By "symbol" I mean a thing that speaks beyond its own particularity, so "symbol" here signifies one thing that says many things. While a symbol may *de*note, it always must *con*note. Within this simple definition a symbol is a thing that may or may not stand for itself but that must always stand for something more than itself.[1] Whether to soul or to heart or to mind, whether to intellect or to intuition, whether to change attitudes, to reshape emotions, to impart convictions, or to express ideas, the symbol makes its statement by moving beyond the boundaries of its own character.

Can the name of a person serve as a symbol? The "historical Moses" for instance may denote an individual and stand for himself in all his particularity. But "Moses our rabbi" connotes something that transcends a particular person at a given moment; it is then Moses in relationship to the Torah, so that "Moses our rabbi" connotes God's giving the Torah to Israel. What about an object? The ram's horn *(shofar)* denotes a particular object. But, represented on the floor or wall of a synagogue, the ram's horn connotes (and may evoke) sentiments, intuitions, feelings, or propositions that vastly transcend the representation of the hardened prominence on the head of the ram: the binding of Isaac, for one thing; Moriah and the Temple, for a second; the judgment of the New Year; the great trumpet that heralds the coming of the Messiah. In all of these cases the "thing" may or may not stand for itself. But to be symbolic, a "thing" must stand for something beyond itself—many things, that are far beyond itself, as a matter of fact.

What about events? In Song of Songs Rabbah, we have seen that an event may be referred to in a single word, e.g., the sea, Sinai. That word then may occur in a list of things that are not events at all. A symbol, for example, may derive from and stand for an event, which, however crudely represented, will bear self-evident implications that transcend what actually happened on that particular day on which the singular event took place. An event reduced to a sign, such as a battle, becomes symbolic when, to the sign for the battle are attached meanings or consequences that extend far beyond what actually happened or what took place on account of what happened in the battle itself: the signs, here, mere names of places, such as Hastings, Agincourt, Gettysburg, Pearl Harbor, or Midway. In the case of (a) Judaism, as I said, the ram's horn may signify the binding of Isaac, hence a singular event; the penitential season encompassing the New Year, hence a recurrent event; the altar of Moriah, hence the Temple in Jerusalem; and a variety of other things. It can stand, also, for Abraham and Isaac, for a symbol may be a person and a person may be symbolic by exemplifying in himself or herself an obvious attitude, virtue, or value. A gesture, such as kneeling, dancing, a motion of the hand or the head that evokes a particular thought, attitude, or feeling serves as a symbol, or it may have no contents to begin with: an action that bears meaning beyond the physical movement of torso or knee that on its own is inert, neutral, without implicit or self-evident meaning.

In line with what we have read in Song of Songs Rabbah, we proceed to the next logical question: can I identify the rather particular parts of the literary evidence that appear to speak through symbols rather than through sentences? In reading a document, how will I know when a set of things portrayed clearly through words serves to speak not for itself alone but also (or only) beyond itself? The answer to that question derives from certain formal traits of the literary evidence. When I have set forth these traits, I shall be able to explain how, in documents of a given type, some words portray symbols rather than convey propositions: *so that symbolic discourse is underway.* We begin with familiar definitions of operative criteria.

First, symbols represented in words are those things (or signs) that transcend their particularity and signify, that is, deliver a message—verbal or intuitive—beyond themselves. We must distinguish these from the things that in context stand for themselves alone and whose meanings are limited to their own characteristics, e.g., the verbal explanations associated with them, or the specific, explicit messages conveyed along with them.

Second, symbols conveyed in words must represent a highly restricted vocabulary, so that some few words recur in symbolic, as distinct from restricted, senses. Only a few words ought to occur in such a way as to warrant classification as symbolic, as distinct from propositional, discourse.

Third and most importantly, it is necessary to specify why the verbal representation of a symbol functions along with other such verbal representations to make a statement that is of a symbolic, not a propositional or syllogistic, character. There must be a theory to explain—not why a word is symbolic in context—but how sets of such symbols combine to convey meaning in a different medium of thought from that conveyed through propositional constructions of words used in a sense restricted by their own traits or significance. Here, again, I want to identify not the words but the syntax and grammar of symbolic discourse. I think I have accomplished this in the chapters we have examined.

1. There is a particular form for use in conducting symbolic, as distinct from propositional and syllogistic, discourse. It is based upon the repeated citation in disciplined parsing of a verse of scripture and the successive imputation of various meanings, entirely cogent with one another, to each component of that verse. The form requires disciplined repetition of the parsed verse together with presentation of a repertoire of distinct meanings to be imputed to the components of that verse. The parsed verse, then, is explained in terms other than those of the verse when it is not parsed. When parsed, element by element, the verse is given a whole new set of meanings or reference points. And when this process is repeated, these new meanings prove multiple. If not repeated, the form is not present. Not surprisingly, the form involved ordinarily bears a rhetorical signal, "another matter."

2. The key words that are utilized in that "other matter" composite form bear meaning only in combination, having in that context no denotative—for instance, propositional—sense outside of the combination with other such verbal signs.

How is the form just described pertinent to our inquiry into the use of language for the representation of symbols, so that, within the cited form in particular, I can adduce evidence that words are utilized *solely* to portray symbols? Two considerations pertain. First is the matter of repetition, integral to the execution of the form just now introduced. Second, and concommitantly, there is the consideration of a restricted vocabulary, which signals the utilization of a restricted, privileged code.

In the context of the another matter composition, "Moses," "David," or "Israel at the sea" serves no propositional purpose at all—conveying no faith or belief that—as (mere) signs, but are available for combination with other signs into aggregates meant to bear meaning in accord with the syntax and grammar of symbolic discourse. "David" or "Moses" in symbolic discourse bears no determinate meaning at all. When we see "Moses" or "the Exodus" we do not know the subject of the signification that symbolic discourse will set forth, let alone the proposition (if any) that will be laid out. Only in combination does "David" or "Moses" or "shofar" or "menorah" gain any signification at all. And then the sense that is desired by the composer of the discourse will emerge not from the words that are used, but from the combinations that are accomplished: combinations of the (otherwise senseless) parsed components of the verse at hand, along with the (otherwise senseless) symbolic signs that are used.

Whatever the words mean in particular has no bearing upon their utilization in symbolic discourse. We know that is the fact because with the words alone in hand, we cannot predict the range of signification that they will be made to communicate: there is no clear limit to the possibilities of the sign, "David," or "Israel at the sea," when those things stand by themselves. We do not know what they may be permitted to signify and we also do not know what they may not be permitted to signify. In the combinations formed to comprise an "another matter" composition, however, they conform to a syntax and grammar that impose determinate meaning upon them: each joined to the other, sign after sign after sign, bears all together a very specific sense or significance. So it is not only that, viewed one by one, these words that serve in the "another matter" compositions bear meanings that transcend their own particularities. It is the simple fact that, standing alone they have no determinate and conventional predictable meanings, but are opaque. They take on meaning only in combination. These "things" are signs and only signs; they yield symbolic discourse and only that.

The composer of a given "another matter" composition therefore accomplishes his goal through the combinations of things that he assembles to make his point: these things together signify this, not that. It follows that, whether in iconic or verbal form, we deal with signs: words that are used as symbols as much as icons that are used as symbols. Whence significance? In symbolic discourse it must derive from combinations of one kind or another. How do these "things"—iconic, verbal alike—then serve as symbols within the definition offered at the outset? First, as I have stressed, their sense (whether propositional, intuitive, or emotional) transcends their immediate limits; or they have no intrinsic sense at all. Second, their meanings exist only in combination, and not alone. The rules of grammar and syntax of propositional communication do not pertain at all. The words at hand—"the sea," "Sinai," "David," "Abraham," "the Torah"— serve as written-down symbols not in bearing meaning that is transcended but *in bearing no meaning within themselves at all*. In the kind of rhetoric represented by "another matter" composites, very often, verbal representations of symbols are lucid *only as words serving a symbolic purpose.*

What traits will make me deem a word opaque except as a symbol, and then, therefore, in a symbolic structure or combination? I think a word is opaque when it can be used in so many different ways as to lose all specific and particular meaning. Such a word is only symbolic, never able to denote, never even limited as to the things that it can connote. Then it is only in its utilization—that is, as with symbols in iconic form, in function and in context— that the word gains any discursive meaning at all. We now recognize that the same trait of utter opacity characterizes words that stand for persons, such as Abraham or Moses; places, such as Sinai or Jerusalem; things, such as the Torah; events, such as the Exodus or the destruction of the Temple (always: the first, never the second!); or actions, such as those of moral or cultic weight alike. The reason I say so is that when we examine those words on their own, we have no clue whatsoever that will accurately permit us to define their meaning wherever they occur. That fact is shown by the simple experiment of collecting all the lists in which Abraham or the Exodus or the destruction of the Temple take a place. The point that Abraham or the destruction makes in one list—its evidentiary use—has nothing in common with the point that those same matters serve to make in some other list. A sign that can mean anything means nothing determinate, and words whose denotative or even connotative sense we cannot establish in the contexts in which they occur bear significance only in combination, never on their own. The key to deciphering symbolic discourse must lie in knowing the secret of the combinations: Why this with that? Why this not with that?

The identification of how a word may serve as a symbol— connoting a meaning that transcends its own particularity, combining with other such verbal symbols to convey a meaning that emerges other than through syllogistic speech—requires demonstration. I am going to show at length and in rich detail that some few things—again: persons, actions, conceptions, events—in a restricted repertoire and in a clearly defined and conventional manner—serve as signs as they combine and recombine in written evidence of a particular kind. These signs commonly refer to scriptural persons, events, actions, or attitudes. They always combine with parsed verses of scripture. It is in the combination of the opaque symbols in verbal form with the opaque clauses of a verse of scripture that the signification of the whole becomes apparent: that is what is meant by recombinancy.

Symbolic discourse undertaken in verbal form proves recombinant. Only in context, in combinations with other such opaque signs, do symbols represented in verbal form begin to bear meaning, whether propositional, intuitive, or emotional. The sole medium for conveying significance of any kind is to combine otherwise opaque symbols, whether conveyed in words or in iconic representation. The set of objects represented on the wall or floor of a synagogue, a list—e.g., Abraham, Isaac, Jacob, Sinai—made up of words that, in context, do not transcend meaning but have no fixed meaning. These constitute symbolic discourse. Iconic symbols, of course, bear their significance only in combination.[2] But the same is true for those words that serve only as signs, and it takes place, when, in association with the parsed components of a given verse of scripture, the opaque symbols combine to make sense, evoke an attitude, even convey a message. As my example stated in abstract terms has shown, the recombinancy therefore has two aspects: (1) the joining in a single list of several opaque symbols: (2) the joining of those opaque verbal signs with the parsed components of the cited verse of scripture. The combinations are then two and distinct: the recombinancy forms the whole into a single statement, a discourse that is wholly carried on in the syntax and grammar of symbols, not in the syntax and grammar of words.

That is why I claim "Abraham" or "the destruction of the Temple" constitutes not a concept but simply a sign in the form of a word. These are words that are opaque until made lucid by utilization in the syntactic and grammatical ways by which symbolic discourse is carried on, and the meanings imputed to these words derive from the grammar and syntax of their utilization. Just as "king," "child," "murder," or "love" may serve in one sentence to convey one proposition or one sentiment, and in another, a very different proposition or sentiment, so "Abraham" or "Sennacherib," "the pig" or "the lamb" may serve an evidently unlimited range of propositional purposes. Then how are we to interpret "Abraham" or "Sinai" or "the destruction of the Temple?" It can only be the way in which we interpret any other word: in the context defined by syntax and grammar. But in the present sort of evidence, where are we to uncover that context? It can only be in the setting of the "sentences" formed by sets of these symbols that are expressed in the form of words—opaque words, until, like all other words, they are used to make sentences. But the sentences then are comprised of sets of opaque symbols, and to make sense of the word symbols, we have to learn how to decipher the sentences that form intelligible thought from these word symbols, whether propositional, intuitive, or attitudinal. The issue, as with the visual symbols of the synagogue, is the same: *How do things combine? How are we to decipher the combinations?*

I claim that in Song of Songs Rabbah we deal with a work of systematic theology, in an odd idiom of symbolic discourse. Let me conclude by explaining why I find the theology of the Judaism of the dual Torah in this remarkable document. Theology may also address vision and speak in tactile ways; it may utilize a vocabulary of opaque symbol (whether conveyed in visual or verbal media) rather than proposition, and through portraying symbol, theology may affect attitude and emotion, speaking its truth through other media than those of philosophy and proposition. From the time of Martin Buber's *Two Types of Faith,* now nearly four decades ago, people have understood that this other type of theology, the one that lives in attitude and sentiment, and that evokes and demands trust, may coexist, or even compete, with the philosophical type of the discourse of which, in general, we are accustomed.

Because there is not a single sustained theological treatise in the canonical writings of the Judaism of the dual Torah, while we do have a monument to a faith that is choate and subject to fully accessible expression, we must teach ourselves how to describe the theology of this Judaism from its complete, systemic documents. One way of doing so lies in the analysis of symbolism. Some documents utilize certain forms to make theological statements in symbolic discourse, the recombinant symbolic ones such as those examined in the preceding pages. They show the symbolic structure that constitutes the theological statement and message for the Judaism of the dual Torah.

Let me now set forth—out of a different document altogether, one example of a fine statement of the symbolic structure of Judaism—a complete theology, worked out symbolically in verbal form to convey a whole, proportionate, structure. This will serve as an example of the kinds of symbols to be found in general in symbolic verbal discourse. I have chosen it as representative because the character of the passage is comparable to many we have read in these pages. It derives not from Song of Songs Rabbah, but from Genesis Rabbah. I wanted to demonstrate how this same mode of theological expression through verbal symbols transforms a simple sentence, "He saw a well in the field." We see that even when scripture speaks in the simplest way about ordinary things, the whole of Israel's life—historical, supernatural, and domestic—fuse in a remarkable statement. Everything comes together, all at once, in the here and now of time beyond time:

Genesis Rabbah LXX:viii

2   A. "As he looked, he saw a well in the field":

B. Rabbi Hama ben Hanina interpreted the verse in six ways (that is, he divides the verse into six clauses and systematically reads each of the clauses in light of the others and in line with an overriding theme):

C. " 'As he looked, he saw a well in the field' ": this refers to the well [of water in the wilderness (Num. 21:17).

D. " '. . . and lo, three flocks of sheep lying beside it' ": specifically, Moses, Aaron, and Miriam.

E. " '. . . for out of that well the flocks were watered': from there each one drew water for his standard, tribe, and family."

F. "And the stone upon the well's mouth was great":

G. Said Rabbi Hanina, "It was only the size of a little sieve."

H. [Reverting to Hama's statement:] " '. . . and put the stone back in its place upon the mouth of the well' ": for the coming journeys. [Thus the first interpretation applies the passage at hand to the life of Israel in the wilderness.]

3   A. " 'As he looked, he saw a well in the field' ": refers to Zion.

B. " '. . . and lo, three flocks of sheep lying beside it' ": refers to the three festivals.

C. " '. . . for out of that well the flocks were watered' ": from there they drank of the Holy
Spirit.

D. " '. . . The stone on the well's mouth was large':
this refers to the rejoicing of the house of the
water drawing."

E. Said Rabbi Hoshaiah, "Why is it called 'the
house of the water drawing'? Because from there
they drink of the Holy Spirit."

F. [Resuming Hama ben Hanina's discourse:] " '. . .
and when all the flocks were gathered there':
coming from 'the entrance of Hamath to the
brook of Egypt' " (1 Kgs. 8:66).

G. " '. . . the shepherds would roll the stone from
the mouth of the well and water the sheep' ":
for from there they would drink of the Holy
Spirit.

H. " '. . . and put the stone back in its place upon the
mouth of the well' ": leaving it in place until the
coming festival. [Thus the second interpretation
reads the verse in light of the Temple celebration
of the Festival of Tabernacles.]

4   A. " '. . . As he looked, he saw a well in the field' ":
this refers to Zion.

B. " '. . . and lo, three flocks of sheep lying beside
it' ": this refers to the three courts, concerning
which we have learned in the Mishnah: There
were three courts there, one at the gateway of the
Temple mount, one at the gateway of the court-
yard, and one in the chamber of the hewn stones
[M. San. 11:2].

C. " '. . . for out of that well the flocks were watered' ": for from there they would hear the
ruling.

D. " 'The stone on the well's mouth was large' ": this
refers to the high court that was in the chamber
of the hewn stones.

E. " '. . . and when all the flocks were gathered
there' ": this refers to the courts in session in the
land of Israel.

F. " '. . . the shepherds would roll the stone from the mouth of the well and water the sheep' ": for from there they would hear the ruling.

G. " '. . . and put the stone back in its place upon the mouth of the well': for they would give and take until they had produced the ruling in all the required clarity." [The third interpretation reads the verse in light of the Israelite institution of justice and administration.]

5   A. " 'As he looked, he saw a well in the field' ": this refers to Zion.

B. " '. . . and lo, three flocks of sheep lying beside it' ": this refers to the first three kingdoms [Babylonia, Media, Greece].

C. " '. . . for out of that well the flocks were watered' ": for they enriched the treasures that were laid upon up in the chambers of the Temple.

D. " '. . . The stone on the well's mouth was large' ": this refers to the merit attained by the patriarchs.

E. " '. . . and when all the flocks were gathered there' ": this refers to the wicked kingdom, which collects troops through levies over all the nations of the world.

F. " '. . . the shepherds would roll the stone from the mouth of the well and water the sheep' ": for they enriched the treasures that were laid upon up in the chambers of the Temple.

G. " '. . . and put the stone back in its place upon the mouth of the well' ": in the age to come the merit attained by the patriarchs will stand [in defense of Israel]. [So the fourth interpretation interweaves the themes of the Temple cult and the domination of the four monarchies.]

6   A. " 'As he looked, he saw a well in the field' ": this refers to the Sanhedrin.

B. " '. . . and lo, three flocks of sheep lying beside it' ": this alludes to the three rows of disciples of sages that would go into session in their presence.

C. " 'for out of that well the flocks were watered' ":

for from there they would listen to the ruling of the law.

D. " '. . . The stone on the well's mouth was large' ": this refers to the most distinguished member of the court, who determines the law decision.

E. " '. . . and when all the flocks were gathered there' ": this refers to disciples of the sages in the land of Israel.

F. " '. . . the shepherds would roll the stone from the mouth of the well and water the sheep' ": for from there they would listen to the ruling of the law.

G. " '. . . and put the stone back in its place upon the mouth of the well': for they would give and take until they had produced the ruling in all the required clarity." [The fifth interpretation again reads the verse in light of the Israelite institution of legal education and justice.]

7   A. " 'As he looked, he saw a well in the field' ": this refers to the synagogue.

B. " '. . . and lo, three flocks of sheep lying beside it' ": this refers to the three who are called to the reading of the Torah on weekdays.

C. " '. . . for out of that well the flocks were watered' ": for from there they hear the reading of the Torah.

D. " '. . . The stone on the well's mouth was large' ": this refers to the impulse to do evil.

E. " '. . . and when all the flocks were gathered there' ": this refers to the congregation.

F. " '. . . the shepherds would roll the stone from the mouth of the well and water the sheep' ": for from there they hear the reading of the Torah.

G. " '. . . and put the stone back in its place upon the mouth of the well': for once they go forth [from the hearing of the reading of the Torah] the impulse to do evil reverts to its place." [The sixth and last interpretation turns to the twin themes of the reading of the Torah in the synagogue and the evil impulse, temporarily driven off through hearing the Torah.]

Genesis Rabbah LXX:ix

1   A. Rabbi Yohanan interpreted the statement in terms of Sinai:

B. " 'As he looked, he saw a well in the field' ": this refers to Sinai.

C. " '... and lo, three flocks of sheep lying beside it' ": these stand for the priests, Levites, and Israelites.

D. " '... for out of that well the flocks were watered' ": for from there they heard the Ten Commandments.

E. " '... The stone on the well's mouth was large' ": this refers to the presence of God.

F. "... and when all the flocks were gathered there":

G. Rabbi Simeon ben Judah of Kefar Akum in the name of Rabbi Simeon: "All of the flocks of Israel had to be present, for if any one of them had been lacking, they would not have been worthy of receiving the Torah."

H. [Returning to Yohanan's exposition:] " '... the shepherds would roll the stone from the mouth of the well and water the sheep' ": for from there they heard the Ten Commandments.

I. " '... and put the stone back in its place upon the mouth of the well': 'You yourselves have seen that I have talked with you from heaven' " (Ex. 20:19).

The six themes read in response to the verse are as follows: (1) Israel in the wilderness; (2) the Temple cult on festivals with special reference to Tabernacles; (3) the judiciary and government; (4) the history of Israel under the four kingdoms; (5) the life of sages; and (6) the ordinary folk and the synagogue. The whole is an astonishing repertoire of fundamental themes of the life of the nation of Israel: at its origins in the wilderness, in its cult, in its institutions based on that cult, in the history of the nations, and, finally, in the twin social estates of sages and ordinary folk, matched by the institutions of the circle of master disciples and the synagogue. The vision of Jacob at the well thus encompassed the whole of the social reality of Jacob's people, Israel. Yohanan's exposition adds what was left out, namely, reference to the revelation of the Torah at Sinai.

The reason I have offered the present passage as a fine instance of symbolic discourse is now clear. If we wished a catalogue of the kinds of topics addressed in passages of symbolic, as distinct from propositional, discourse, the present catalogue proves compendious and complete. And now, in this abstract from a different compilation altogether, we see what has happened in the pages of our document in a vast and systematic and orderly way. A religion that makes its statement through what people do—the food they eat, the clothes they wear, the attitudes they express through word and deed—can find no more appropriate medium of speech than symbolic discourse. Given what that religion wants to say, our sages can have chosen no more appropriate book of scripture than Song of Songs. In the words of Aqiba, "For the entire age is not so worthy as the day on which the Song of Songs was given to Israel. For all the scriptures are holy, but the Song of Songs is holiest of all." Now we know why.

To conclude, let us revert to our starting point: the notion that in this document we examine the theology of the Judaism of the dual Torah. Have I claimed too much? For all we have seen is discrete statements joined to a verse of scripture, long lists of this and that. What sort of theology does our document set forth, if any?

Although theology may comprise propositions that are well crafted into a cogent structure about fundamental questions of God and revelation, the social entity that realizes that revelation, the attitudes and deeds that God, through revelation, requires of humanity—there are entirely other ways. And here we have seen that other way: a theology that comes to realization in feeling, sentiment, emotion, and attitude, and also in propositions, syllogisms, arguments, and evidence. Judaism is a religion that conducts a love affair with God, and in such a love affair, people do not describe the one they love, so much as express their feelings for the one they love. The theology of Judaism, as our document portrays it, expresses itself in images of love, because that is the only language—a language of emotion and sentiment rather than proposition and argument—this Judaism can speak at all. Just as it finds truth in the here and now of everyday life and states its truths that way, so it finds love in the sequences of images that evoke deep feeling.

Theology—the structure and system, the perception of order and meaning of God, in God, through God—these may make themselves known otherwise than through the media of thought and expression that yield belief. Theology can deliver its message through sentiment and emotion, through heart as much as mind. It can be conviction as much as position, and conviction for its part is orderly, proportioned, compelling of mind and intellect by reason of right attitude rather than right proposition or position. That is to say, theology may set forth a system of thought in syllogistic arguments concerning the normative truths of the world view, social entity, and way of life of a religious system. But theology may speak other than in dynamic and compelling argument, and theologians may accomplish their goal of speaking truth about God other than through the statements made by language and in conformity with the syntax of reasoned thought.

At this very early stage in thinking through this method of theological description, it suffices to say that the Midrash-compilations presented here and in the other volumes of the Library of the Bible of Judaism, Lamentations Rabbah, Esther Rabbah I, and Ruth Rabbah, make theological statements. These statements are not episodic but systematically presented. They are repeated over and over again, and it is to make these statements that the documents cited are constituted. That is the difference between a document of theological discourse and one that is, instead, of philosophical genre, purpose, and character. These compilations, all of them generally regarded as belonging in the same age as the Babylonian Talmud make theological, only theological, and only a few theological statements.

Notes

1. But, as I shall argue in the following pages, a verbal symbol that denotes is less symbolic than an opaque verbal symbol, one that connotes but does not denote anyting in particular. That observation will be central to my argument in this chapter and to part 1 of the analysis of evidence.

2. I have discussed that matter at length in my *Symbol and Theology in Judaism* (Minneapolis: Augsburg-Fortress Press, 1992).

General Index

Abba ben Rabbi Kahana
  ark of the Torah, 77
  words of scribes as precious as
  Torah, 50
Abbahu
  dove and olive leaf for Noah, 91
  throne of glory, 83
  word from the mouth of God, 39
Abun, ark of the Torah, 80
Aha
  Mezuzah and holy life, 71
  Solomon and seat of authority,
  24
Aibu, sisterhood and peace of God,
  104
Ammi, ark of the Torah, 79
Aqiba, on uncleanness, 3
Ark of the Torah, 76–78
Azariah
  ark of the Torah, 77, 81–82
  commandments as revelation of
  love, 28, 33, 37, 40
  seat of authority, presence of
  God, 75

Bar Qappara, sisterhood and peace
  of God, 100
Ben Azzai, on uncleanness, 3
Berekhiah
  daughters of Jerusalem, role of,
  64–65
  love and jealousy, 97
  sisterhood and peace of God, 99

  throne of glory, 83
  word from mouth of God, 32
Bibi
  ark of the Torah, 77
  daughters of Jerusalem, role of,
  64
Brotherhood and family, 93–94
Buber, Martin, *Two Types of Faith,*
  116, 123
Bun, throne of glory, 83

Cleanness and atonement, 66
Comely: *See* Faithfulness
Commandments
  performance of, 85–91
  protection of Israel, 42

Dark side, failures of Israel, 59–68
Daughters of Jerusalem, women as
  builders of Jerusalem, 63–66
Divinity of God, acceptance of, 27
Doves
  innocence and faithfulness,
  87–88
  olive leaf for Noah, 90–91

Eighteen benedictions, and holy
  life, 70–72
Eliezer ben Jacob, cleanness and
  atonement, 67

Faithfulness, successes of Israel,
  59–68

125

Index of Biblical
and Talmudic References